# Curling Past and Present

# CURLING

# PAST and

# PRESENT

*by*

# W. A. CREELMAN

### B. A., LL. D.

*Including*

*An Analysis of the*
*Art of Curling*

*by*

## H. E. Weyman

McClelland & Stewart Limited
Publishers      Toronto
1950

Printed in Canada by
T. H. Best Printing Company, Limited

*To*
*My Wife, Isabel,*
*Once An Active Curler*

*Toast her ye sons o' the stane and the broom—*
*She's a poem in motion as swaying and whirling*
*She rides on undaunted to victory or doom*
*The Verra Soul O' The Game—The Spirit O' Curling.*

# Acknowledgment

Special thanks are due to a large group, mostly curlers, for the help freely given in the compiling of this book. It is, of course, impossible to mention more than a very few of those to whom I am indebted:

I should like to thank Messrs. Douglas & Foulis, Publishers, Edinburgh, and the Royal Caledonian Curling Club for their permission to make free use of the material contained in John Kerr's HISTORY OF CURLING; Judge Patterson of New Glasgow, Nova Scotia, Captain of the All-Canadian Curling Team that visited Scotland in 1920-21, for his critical examination of the manuscript; Messrs. E. C. MacKinnon of Cranbrook, British Columbia, J. C. Loucks of Calgary, Alberta, and H. P. Webb of Halifax, Nova Scotia, for their prompt and detailed replies to many an anxious query; Mr. William Brown of the Granite Curling Association, Montreal, for information as to the use of irons in Quebec; Mr. Glen Harris of Superior, Wisconsin, editor of the only paper in the world devoted solely to curling, for kindly forwarding material of great value on curling in the North Western United States; Mr. Albert Shaw, Jr., Ardsley-On-Hudson, New York, Mr. F. A. Hartney of Mount Hope, New York, Mr. John M. Macrae of Detroit, Michigan, for information on curling "Owre the Border", and Miss Marion Knox of Sydney for kind assistance with the illustration of the book.

# CONTENTS

# Foreword

The idea of writing this book first came to me a good many years ago. That nothing was done until fate intervened was probably due to the fact that I spent most of my leisure hours playing rather than writing about the grand and glorious game. As to my suitability for the task of a chronicler of curling, I don't think it is presumption on my part to consider myself a veteran. As far back as the season of 1902-03, I had had many years of active play behind me, and indeed that winter captained a team from Cape Breton against a fine group of Scottish curlers who, led by Dr. John Kerr, were then visiting our country on their first official tour. The book remained unwritten and I continued to curl through the years until, in the early thirties, I suffered a severe fall on the ice. The doctors decided that I should never curl again. Although it was a cruel blow to be denied further participation in my beloved game, it was then that I first found time to undertake this book.

While visiting in Edinburgh during the summer of 1937 I thought to take advantage of my stay by attempting to collect some data concerning the origin and early progress of the game in Scotland. On making enquiries I was informed that all that was known of the early history of the game had already appeared in a volume entitled HISTORY OF CURL-ING by Dr. John Kerr. I was able to obtain a copy of this admirable work, although it had been out of print for many years, and found it to be everything that one could desire as a history of the game. And yet, a perusal of this work in no way

15

diminished my wish to prepare my own book, for I considered that Dr. Kerr's work was too long and too detailed for the average curler of this generation. And too, I wanted to write from the point of view of the Canadian and American curler, so I returned home determined to make a survey of the game in our own country.

The volume now before you is the result of my endeavours. Although the book is not as complete in scope as I had hoped to make it I do think there will be something of interest to every curler interested in the lore and romance of the game's history, in its progress during the last century on this continent, and in the analysis of recommended playing techniques. I am, of course, indebted to Dr. John Kerr's book for the material presented in Part One: Scottish Origins. I gratefully acknowledge the indulgence of the Royal Caledonian Curling Club, and of the publishers, in permitting me to make free use of this material. Without their assistance it would have been impossible for me to trace the early history of the game.

In Part Two: North American Curling, I have attempted a survey of the progress of the game on this continent. The facts presented have been marshalled only after some years spent imposing on the good nature and kindness of scores of club and association secretaries. It is regrettable that these records are not more complete. Many old documents have been destroyed by fire and other natural hazards. And too, the remarkable shortage of records bears mute testimony to the fact that the curlers in this country have always been more concerned with doing than recording. The history, as presented, is accurate as far as I have been able to ascertain. That some keen, keen curlers will uncover errors in the whole I have no doubt. I would like to hear from them, and if they are able to substantiate their claims I shall make corrections in the next edition of this book, for my sole desire is to see the story of our glorious game accurately recorded.

In Part Three: The Modern Game, I thought it desirable to discuss modern methods and techniques of play for those interested in improving their game but more particularly for those who are just now taking up the broom for the first time. After some consideration I decided that curling could be no better served than by enlisting the aid of my good friend Mr. H. E. Weyman of Levis, Quebec. When asked if he would furnish some material, he readily consented. Part Three contains, therefore, the core of his years of experience and research into the best methods and techniques of play. This material has already appeared in more detail in his well-known handbook *An Analysis of the Art of Curling*. I deem it a privilege to present it again between the covers of this book.

I have said that this volume does not cover the subject in all its phases to the extent that I had hoped, for limitations of both time and space have been imposed. One facet of curling today that deserves more space is Ladies' curling. When we consider the long centuries during which curling has never been thought of save as a man's game, such an upheaval as that of allowing "the Wimmin" to curl was regarded at first as not very far removed from revolutionary. I can vividly recall that long-ago meeting of the club to which I then belonged when this matter was first submitted to the members. A gallant few were in favour; but the great majority were decidedly hostile.

Many members were apprehensive of feminine interference not only in their own enjoyment of the game but also in the liberty of a long-established association. So the answer sent back to the fair applicants was to the effect that if the rink were ever to be made free to the ladies, it would only be to the wives, sweethearts and sisters of the curlers themselves. Thirty-seven long years ago, that was!

But by slow degrees the members of curling clubs began yielding not only to plain justice but to a still plainer common

sense, until Ladies' Curling Clubs are now successfully functioning in a goodly number of cities and towns all the way
from Edinburgh to Vancouver. And what has been the consequence? The only consequence has been an additional
exemplification of the principle: The greatest good for the
greatest number.

Our lady curlers, however welcome they may become,
will never be looked upon as a handy reserve force to fill up
recurring gaps in club membership. Our school boys, on the
other hand, will not only make up reserve forces but in
addition will receive much valuable training in the way of
team discipline and unquestioned obedience to orders as
eventually to make them better all-round citizens than they
might otherwise have been.

In fine, the oft-proven fact that early training of the right
kind so frequently leads to the very highest proficiency, both
in one's calling and in one's games, should long ago have
prompted a practical course in curling for school boys. The
training of youth is the one sure foundation on which to build
a great game and a great nation. Discipline and character-
building are essentials in both. It has been emphasized by
many educational authorities that the national and provincial
school curling is doing much to produce the right type of
Canadian citizen. The growing interest in boys' curling is
therefore a most heartening development. What started as a
Western Canada High School Curling Championship at
Regina, in 1947, has blossomed into the increasingly successful Canadian High School Curling Championship, held
at Winnipeg in 1948, Edmonton in 1949 and Quebec City
in 1950.

A true history of curling should of course go beyond the
British Isles, Canada and the United States. Several other
countries in Europe have taken up the game. In Switzerland,
the keen desire to attract more winter tourists explains why
St. Moritz, in addition to her skating and skiing, has for some

years been a home of curling. And there they have curling outdoors under magnificent conditions.

In the sixties of the last century a curling club called "The Elverhae" functioned in Norway for a year before dying out: yet during the present post-war period, somewhat surprisingly, the game has come back there, and this time seemingly to stay. Also, during the same sixties, three attempts were made by Scotchmen to transplant curling from their own land to Russia, the last attempt being made by Lord Dufferin during his stay at St. Petersburg while serving as British Ambassador at the court of the Czar. His plan even included the erection of a spacious building to house a rink. But the Russians did no more than look on; and today their descendants live behind an iron curtain. Russia's neighbour, Sweden, however, is following the example of Norway during this post-war period in succumbing to the lure of the broom and the stone.

In the Southern Hemisphere, New Zealand is the only country that has taken up curling as yet. There it is confined to one province, Otago, and the association comprises fifteen clubs. The bonspiels are usually held outdoors and under conditions almost as spectacular as those that prevail in Switzerland. The game will undoubtedly spread to Australia, and who knows, from there possibly to the remaining portions of the great frost zone of the Southern Hemisphere.

This is the story of what is perhaps the world's greatest game. It has been possible to show, I hope, that curling has an uplifting influence on the character of its devotees, and does its part in binding peoples together in the bonds of lasting goodwill. In fine, the book may actually lead a reader to believe that curlers "ivery whaur" are ladies and gentlemen. What more could be asked!

W. A. Creelman

Sydney, Nova Scotia,
October 9th, 1950.

# PART ONE

# Scottish Origins

# CHAPTER I

# THE ORIGIN OF CURLING

*Then drain deep the cog till the brain is a-whirling*
*And pledge me ye lovers of Scotia's ain game*
*To the memory of him—the inventor of curling*
*Though the mists of oblivion envelop his name.*

A WISE SCOT has well reasoned that wherever there was ice there must have been games on ice, and by successive experimental stages one of these games finally evolved into the greatest ice sport which man enjoys today—curling. There have been more or less plausible conjectures as to the origin of this outstanding game. But unfortunately, conjectures are not proofs, so the point remains unsettled.

The first *History of Curling*, published in 1811, was the work of a Scottish divine, The Reverend John Ramsay of Gladsmuir; the second, a *Historical Sketch of Curling* was written by H. Crawford of Kilmarnock in 1828; while the third, published in 1890, was written by another Scottish divine, The Reverend John Kerr, whom a number of Canadian and American curlers may still remember as having been both the chaplain and the captain of that splendid band of Scottish Knights of the Broom which visited Canada and the United States during the winter of 1902-3. Dr. Kerr's *History of Curling* contains practically all that was known of the game's origin up to the end of the last century. He said:

23

. . . it is as well, however, to bear in mind that while it is a
game of great antiquity, and can be traced back for nearly
400 years, it was only about the middle of the last century
that it began to take on the dignity of a truly national game.
Unlike its neighbour—golf, which, barring the *gutta,* has been
played in much the same form from the beginning, and unlike
lawn tennis, which is simply the revival of a game played
centuries ago in a form that required as much skill as the
present — curling has so completely developed out of its
ancient mode, that it is only by the help of an evolutionary
theory, which requires great faith on our part, that we can
trace connection between the modern and the ancient game.
Since the game, through the rounding of the stone fully a
century ago, made such a break away from the style of previous centuries, its progress has been remarkable.

Researchers into the history of curling have tried to
ascertain what the oldest forms of the game were as well
as to find out when, where, and how each and all of its many
phases have come into existence. They attacked the problem
in three distinct ways: first, by noting the different shapes
and weights of those crude monstrosities which were doubtless prized and well beloved "channel-stanes" once upon a
time; second, by attempting to trace the origin of words
used in ice games both in Scotland and elsewhere; and third,
by way of reasonable assumption.

Ramsay laid great stress on the extreme likelihood of
the desired knowledge being brought to light through tracing
the origin of words peculiar to curling. He held that if a
majority of such words could be shown to be of either Dutch
or German derivation then it might be claimed that the game
likewise had its origin either in the Low Countries or in
Germany.

After conferring at length with such of his contemporaries as were familiar with both philology and curling,
Ramsay concluded that, in an unrecorded long ago, the art
of curling had been imported to Scotland from the Continent
and could in no wise be regarded as native in origin. Dr.

Kerr quoted Ramsay's own words on this point to show plainly where he finally stood:

> We have all the evidence which etymology can give in favour of its Continental origin. The terms, being all Dutch or German, point to the Low Countries as the place at which it most probably originated, or, at least, from whence it was conveyed to us. For if it were not introduced from the Continent, but was first invented in this country, it must have been at a time when German and Low Dutch were the prevailing languages. Now, though the Saxon was once pretty general in this country, and there are still many Dutch words in our language, yet those German dialects were never so general as to make it credible that our countrymen, in any particular invention, would employ them alone as the appropriate terms. In the history of inventions, such a phenomenon is not to be found. Had there been only one or two foreign terms, these would not have militated much against the domestic origin of the game, but *the whole of the terms being Continental, compel us to ascribe to it a Continental origin.*

Dr. Kerr sharply dissented from such a view, arguing that etymology was too much like curling itself—a slippery game that could not be depended on over-much to furnish historical data. He admitted that the curler's language as he played the game was peculiar, and that anyone unacquainted with curling might suppose it to be foreign; but he asserted that despite its strange use of words and phrases, it was essentially native.

Dr. Kerr concluded that actually Ramsay buttressed his foreign origin theory largely on a dictionary, the work of one Dr. Jamieson, dealing with words especially used in Scotland. He found that although Jamieson's work was an acknowledged storehouse for the student of Scottish literature, many of its statements on origins were suggestive rather than positive. As, for instance, Jamieson's conclusions as to the Continental origins of such stock curling terms as the very word *curl* itself, along with the adjective *curling*, and finally, the word *rink*. He found that Ramsay suggested, without at-

tempting to establish the fact, that *curl* was a derivative of
the German *kurzweil*, meaning an amusement, a game; and
that *curling* could thus logically be claimed as the derivative
of the German verb *kurzweillen*, meaning "to play for amusement." While as to the word *rink*, Ramsay thought it to be a
derivative of the ancient Saxon, *hrink*, meaning a strong man.

But in considering such a key word as *rink*, even a person lacking a knowledge of philology might well ask just
what logical connection there could be between a curling
rink with its ice-cut circles around the tee and this Saxon
word *hrink*, a strong man, even though the last four letters
do happen to make up the spelling of *rink*.

On the other hand, an Anglo-Saxon glossary lists the
word *hring*, meaning a circle, a ring. Surely the connection of
the word *hring*, with a curling rink and its circles would seem
to be much too obvious for it to be set aside for the word
*hrink*.

Dr. Jamieson also mentioned the word *kuting* (also
spelled *quoiting* or *coiting*) as well as two words listed in an
ancient work on etymology, a *Teutonic Dictionary*, by Kilian,
published in 1632—*kluyten* (to play with lumps or balls,
frozen) and *kalluyten* (to contend with quoits on an icy
plain) in defence of his theory that curling was of Continental origin.

Jamieson held that *kuting* or *quoiting* were once names
given to curling, due to the fact that in its primitive form
curling was somewhat allied to quoit pitching. The old
fingers-and-thumb-holed curling stones were swung from
behind and then, well-floored, were sent gliding down the
ice at a fixed mark. These primitive stones received the general name "channel" from being taken from the rock-strewn
beds of rivers or brooks, and at first had no handles but only
holes or hollows cut out for grasping. The very fact of their
being called *quoits* led Jamieson to voice the wishful query:
"Can it be supposed that *quoits* has been softened from the

Teutonic *kluyten?*" It would have been more to the point
had he asked, "Can it be *proved?*"

Of course, any terms used in curling which are even
faintly suggestive of being Dutch or German in origin cannot be ignored altogether, as appearing to militate against
the game being of native origin. Curling terms used both
before and during Ramsay's time have in many instances,
as Dr. Kerr admitted, a foreign look about them. But
Jamieson's theory concerning the word *coit* gave his trustful
disciple, Ramsay, little grounds to regard it, as he so eagerly
did, as further proof that all the evidence of etymology is in
favour of the foreign origin of curling. In fact, what evidence
there is would seem to show that for long generations the
majority of such words have been regarded as probably
native to the soil of Scotland, as all who are sufficiently
informed can see for themselves in the following lists:

| *Native Words* | | *Foreign or Doubtful* |
|---|---|---|
| boardhead | hack | bonspiel |
| channel-stone | hatch | brough |
| chuckle | hog | colly |
| coalscore | rack | curl |
| cock | skip | kuting |
| cockee | stug | quoiting (coiting) |
| cramp | tee | rink |
| crampit | toesee | wick |
| director | tramp | witter |
| draw | tricker | wittyr |

A Scottish authority, one of Ramsay's correspondents,
J. B. Greenshields, in his *Annals of the Parish Lesmahagow,*
contributed the following in the matter of the foreign origin
of curling:

> That foreigners in considerable numbers settled in our
> country is an undoubted historical fact; but, as the most skil-
> ful philologists pronounce the German, Danish, Swedish

and the ancient Saxon to be all of Gothic origin, and that
the English language is mainly composed of these, it does
seem unwarrantable, from etymology alone, and in the
absence of historical proof, to decide upon the foreign origin
of the game, seeing that our ancestors could not avoid
using words of foreign derivation. "The whole fabric and
scheme of the English language," says that great authority,
Dr. Johnson, "is Gothic or Teutonic."

Also, a Professor Masson, whose opinion Dr. Kerr valued
highly, had this to say:

> I see no proof in them collectively (i.e. the curling words)
> that the game came from the Continent. Most of the terms
> are of Teutonic origin in a general way: some are of French
> original; some might even be claimed as of Celtic original;
> and a few seem recent inventions . . . of players of the game
> within the last century or so, to define recurring circum-
> stances and incidents of the game previously unnamed.
>    I do not think much can be made of your (Dr. Kerr's)
> question on either side by chasing up etymologies. The mat-
> ter seems mainly a *historical* one.
>    . . . The question is whether the particular game of
> curling can be proved to have been in use anywhere out of
> Scotland . . . If it ever existed anywhere else, it ought to be
> found in that place now; for the ice still remaining, the extinc-
> tion of the game, if once in use, may be voted as impossible.
> Curlers, therefore ought to drive at this question, "is there
> any curling now, or anything like curling anywhere in the
> world out of Scotland, except by obvious and provable deriva-
> tion from Scotland?"

A Professor Mackinnon also contributed his quota to
the general argument:

> The great majority of the words are not only Teutonic, but
> seem to me to be native. *Hack*, e.g. is an old English verb,
> and a noun used in the same sense is but what may be looked
> for. On the other hand, *bonspiel* is foreign, and is made up
> of *bon* (Fr.) and a form of the Teutonic *spielen*. I may say
> that in the West Highlands we have borrowed *spel* from the
> Norsemen in the same sense of "a game." *Rink*, evidently
> the same as ring, looks a loan from the Continent, though
> the Scotch often pronounce their medials pretty strongly,

perhaps under Continental and Highland influences. On the general question: if the words were proved foreign, the presumption would be a strong one, that the game was imported—so strong indeed that it would "hold the field" until a native origin was proved by other evidence. But my knowledge does not enable me to say with any degree of confidence that the words you quote, or many of them, are borrowed into Scotch.

Captain Crawford, the author of *Sixty-six Years of Curling*, the same being *Records of the North Woodside Curling Club 1820-1886*, presented his opinions in a capital piece of evolutionary logic as follows:

We believe that the game originated among rural workers and the tillers of the land in those moorland districts where undrained lochs and tarns were numerous centuries ago. Let us suppose a hard frost sets in: the rural labourer finds his plough frozen in the furrow; the earth is hard as iron; everything is bound in the close embrace of the Frost King; the rural workers meet together in their enforced idleness; the exhilarating weather acts like a stimulant on their spirits and the country folk are full of fun; the loch and stream are frozen; they venture on the ice for the purpose of sliding; one mirthful fellow seizes a boulder; he putts it along the ice and he and his fellows are astonished at the distance it is carried on the smooth surface of the frozen waters; he challenges his companions to a test of strength and (thus) they begin (from time to time) to select suitable stones from the beds of the rivers and from the dry stone dykes, and play one against the other by hurling the stones along in rude fashion. Ultimately, they fix a mark at which the stone is to be thrown and in process of time the game becomes developed into an exhilarating pastime. The rude stone selected, from its natural adaption for playing, soon becomes moulded into more fitting form; it is chipped to a shape; its undersurface is polished, a rude handle or grip is inserted; and the enjoyment afforded in bright winter days by meeting together in this friendly rivalry bring out the whole rural population to enjoy the fun. The farmer and the ploughman keep themselves in good humour during the forced idleness of winter; the village workers find their labours impeded by the frost as well as the ploughman. The smith is unemployed because all farm and rural labour is suspended and he joins in the fun and frolic of the game. The joiner and the artisan of the district catch the infection and play sides against one another. The laird and the parish priest enter into the enjoyment and encourage the innocent and exhilarating pastime which has many salutary social influences and keeps the hands of the people out of mischief. If the frost continues for long periods, as it often does on the upland districts of Scotland, one hamlet challenges another to a game of Curling, as was also their wont in olden days to challenge each other to games of shinty, football and the like. Thus the game grew into district and national importance and the implements of the sport—rude and primitive at first—have been developed into handsome and fitting accessories of the exhilarating recreation.

Though lacking Captain Crawford's intimate knowledge of living conditions in the rural Scotland of the time, I have often pondered over the origin of this grand game, usually arriving at the conclusions so logically worked out by him.

Weighing all these testimonies for and against the idea of curling being of foreign origin, Dr. Kerr, in his splendid history thus summed up:

(1) That the proportion of the words of Teutonic origin in the curling vocabulary has been over-estimated.

(2) That even if a great many are Teutonic it does not follow that the game of curling must have had its origin in the Low Countries.

However, it is not impossible that the Scottish word, *curling*, the German *kluyten* and the Icelandic *knattleikr* (of which more specific mention will be made later on) are all descendants of a common ancestor game. As an instance, the Dutch had two ice games, one a kind of shinty played on the ice with snowballs; while the other was a kind of pitching game played with small quoits. But as has previously been stated, the German word *kluyten* has also been shown as respectively designating just such games. Again, Dr. Kerr pointed out that ice games have also been played in countries north as well as south of Scotland, and that the Icelanders, for instance, had a game called *knattleikr*, played upon ice by means of what were called bowls. Such a parentage of curling, he thought, was quite as feasible as the Continental one on etymological grounds; he related that it no longer existed, and concluded that its relationship to curling must have been very distant.

Dr. Kerr continued on this important point as to origin, by quoting from a description of an ice game a Thomas Purdie participated in on an artificial ice pond near Munich, Bavaria. Presumably this was in 1848, for the description appeared in the *Annual* of the Royal Caledonian Curling Club for that year. Purdie wrote:

> I was not content with a mere verbal description of . . . the game as there practiced . . . but played a game on a barn floor with the man who takes charge of the Pond and Curling stone, and vindicated the honour of Scotland by beating him with his own weapons and on his own ground. The game is a very ancient one, and is played generally throughout Bavaria, but more especially in the neighbourhood of Munich, the capital. It is common for gentlemen to have within their grounds artificial ponds for the practice of the game. These consist generally of one rink, fifty or sixty yards long, which is the common length between the Tees. The Tees, called Taube, are moveable, and the nearest stone counts wherever the Tee may be moved to. They are formed of square pieces of wood four inches long by two thick. The "stones" are made of wood, and are, in German, called "ice sticks", for an equally good reason that in Scotland we call them stones. . . . Their sticks weigh from 12 to 25 pounds, English; run on a sole of from 10 to 13 inches, encircled close to the sole by a heavy rim of iron, to give weight and solidity. The handle is perpendicular, about nine inches long and slightly curved at the top. There are from two to four players a side. Numbered balls are put in a box and each man takes his side according to the number of his ball. The places of the players are fixed by playing one end and each man ranks according to the distance his stick measures from the Tee . . . The sides do not play alternately as with us; but when one side has the shot, the other must play till they take it out. . . . When all

Fig. I   The Ice Stick.

the sticks are played . . . the party gaining the end counts
six. . . . The stakes are paid at the end of each game, and
there is always some stake played for. The rinks played on
are at least ten yards longer than with us, and it must require
considerable force to propel the sticks. They are swung back-
wards and forwards in the hand before being thrown off.
You will see, however, from the above, that it has little in
common with our roaring game—no wicking, guarding, or
running a port; and, famed as Bavaria is for its brooms and
broom girls, there is even no sweeping, so that their game
is child's play compared to our noble science.

Given a cold climate where a man must exercise himself
to keep his blood warm, an inherent tendency from Old
Adam to throw stones, and a sheet of ice to disport upon,
we have all the makings of our national game without having
to search far for its origin.

Incidentally, here is an historical note about one feature
of curling which is an absolute essential to the game as we
know it today. That is, the out-or-in-turn impulse given to
the stone at delivery. Dr. Kerr concluded that the secret of
this twist was discovered "long before the end of the eight-
teenth century", but that it came to be known as the Fenwick
Twist in the first year of the nineteenth century. A poem,
said to have been composed, extempore, on the occasion of
a match, in 1784, between the Duke of Hamilton and M'Dowall of Castlesemple, contains a stanza which lends some
weight to his conclusion, as follows:

*Six stones within the circle stand,*
*And every port is blocked,*
*But Tam Pate he did TURN THE HAND*
*And soon the port unlocked.*

All curlers of today know that if given an initial in-or-out-turn twist (or call it the "elbow-out" or "elbow-in") the stone on nearing the end of its course (and due to this, losing much of its initial rectilinear impulse) begins (due to its initial curvilinear impulse) to swerve as required to the left or right, thus enabling it to curl around a guard, remove a hitherto protected stone, and lie shot.

All spherical bodies such as cricket and billiard balls, or circular bodies such as curling stones, when gliding along an almost frictionless icy surface, will, if given at the start these two respective impulses, react in practically the same way. For in exact proportion, as the rectilinear impulse begins to die out, will the curvilinear impulse begin to take fuller control—giving us the well known curve of the baseball, the break of the cricket-ball, and the right and left burrow of the curling stone; in each case taking effect just at the time needed. But lacking a knowledge of the law controlling spherical and circular bodies, when moving almost without friction under these simultaneous yet opposing impulses, not one of these games would have ever come into existence.

Not until curlers commenced using partly rounded stones could they have become aware that this better type of stone began noticeably to swerve to the right or left when possessed of an elbow-in, or elbow-out, curvilinear motion. And such a regular happening, once fully perceived, must unquestionably have led those curling forefathers around 1800 to perceive further that the old drive and smash method had had its day, giving place to an almost entirely different game—a world game with possibilities hitherto undreamed of.

It would seem, therefore, that curling as we now know it, was not a matter of invention, but of evolution.

# CHAPTER II

# LANG SYNE REFERENCES TO CURLING IN SCOTTISH HISTORY

*In the days o' lang syne as some auld stories tell us*
*At Yule when the fiels are a' kiver'd wi' snaw;*
*Nae bonspiel was ken'd but the horn brightly sparkling,*
*And wild burst o' joy sounding loud thro' the ha'.*

NOTWITHSTANDING THE VERY NATURAL DESIRE OF MANY modern curlers to find early references to their beloved sport, an extensive period was allowed to lapse before the game was considered sufficiently important to merit even a small share of public recognition. Dr. Kerr stated emphatically that no mention is made of the game of curling by any of our Scottish historians previous to the year 1600.

The first vague mention of curling is to the effect that certain Scottish kings had either favoured or had actually taken part in the game. There is reason to suspect the authenticity of this, however. While there is no question but that James I of Scotland excelled in the manly exercises of throwing the stone and the hammer, in walking and running and horsemanship, yet history has made no mention of him as having been a lover of, or a player at, curling. So also is history silent as to any curling propensities on the part of James II and James III.

Tradition has it that the fourth James showed an interest in curling and ordered a silver model of a curling stone to

34

be made. This was to be played for annually. But neither the silver model nor any official account in the old records of the Lord Treasurer having paid out money for the silver model can be found.

Sir Richard Broun in a second edition of his *Memorabilia Curliana* claimed that curling is referred to in Pitscottie's *Chronicles of Scotland,* 1511-42, wherein an account of certain sports, held in welcome of an English embassy from the court of Henry VIII, is given in detail. These sporting events were ordered by the Scottish king, and his mother, a sister of Henry VIII, was present on that occasion.

Along with other sports such as shooting, leaping wrestling, running and casting the stone, additional mention is made of a *bonspiel* under the special care of the dowager queen, Margaret Tudor, a woman whom history reports to have been more addicted to court intrigues than to the manly sport of curling. This word *bonspiel,* however, must never be taken as being wholly connoted with curling since it is a compound made up of the French word *bon,* good, and the Teutonic *spiel,* a game.

Jamieson in his *Etymological Dictionary of the Scottish Language* really settled the question as to whether *bonspiel* in this instance referred only to curling. He showed that the word *bonspiel,* used to describe one of the sports held in that embassy welcome at St. Andrews in 1530, referred only to archery. And in addition to Jamieson's negative finding there is another point to be considered. Had curling been played at the courts of either James IV or James V mention would surely have been made of it by the contemporary poet, Sir David Lindsay, whose special duty it was to arrange and superintend the royal sports. Yet Sir David penned no rhymes anent curling.

While curling is a right royal and noble game, it can be just as truly said that since its beginning it owes nothing substantial to either king or noble. This may account for the fact that between 1600 and 1700 there were only a few references to persons in connection with curling, but though few, they were genuine.

James VI of Scotland (James I of England), that Royal and learned fool (as he was once termed), was once spoken of in 1844, as a keen, keen curler. This obvious exaggeration came about in this wise; at a regular meeting of a then loyal but prominent Jacobite Society, a toast was proposed in honour of the Prince of Wales:

> He (the Prince) has scarcely begun his education but you will all agree with me in maintaining that if in the progress of that education he is not made a keen, keen curler—if he is not thoroughly initiated into all the mysteries of that health-restoring, strength-renovating, nerve-bracing, blue-devil-expelling, incomparable game of curling—his education will be entirely bungled and neglected. I think that The Royal Grand Club should take that subject into its earliest and most serious consideration. We would all deprecate Royal degeneracy. His ancestors were distinguished for the countenance they gave to the manly and ennobling exercises and pastimes peculiar to Scotland. It is true that some of them—such as James III, James IV and James V—for some time discountenanced some of the amusements for the purpose of encouraging the practice of archery when the country was at war: but James VI rose in all the glory of curling, as well as golfing, grandeur, and greatness; he was not only a distinguished golfer but a "keen, keen curler." He knew how to keep his own side of the rink, to sweep the rink, his neighbour's stone from the score to the tee, his adversary's past it. Let the young Prince go and do likewise.

The early seventeenth century was typical of the many years of religious strife throughout Scotland. The Presbyterians in their Glasgow Assembly of 1638, set King Charles and his Commissioner at defiance, and determined to make a clean sweep of the bishops. But as reports show, instead of sweeping them away just because they happened to be bishops, the Assembly began a series of mock trials attacking their moral characters. The proceedings were faithfully recorded by Robert Baillie, Minister of Kilwinning. Concerning one bishop we find this odd record: "Orkney's process came first before us: he was a curler on the ice on the Sabbath day."

George Graham, for such was the bishop's name, did not make a very good impression by his willingness to renounce episcopacy in the hope of retaining his property, but in other respects he was not as bad as his neighbours. However, commentators of the day record that at that time the Sabbath was regarded as more of a festival than a fast, and that after attending church the members were free to amuse themselves. Dr. Kerr suggests that the good bishop probably joined some of his parishioners and "had a fling" with them, without losing their respect or his own peace of conscience. In any case, the charge came to nothing.

The old-time incident recalls an amusing story of a certain district in Northern Ontario, wholly made up of Scottish immigrants. The minister, one of the strait-laced John Knox type, happened on a bitterly cold Sunday afternoon to be driving with a well-loved elder for the purpose of visiting an ailing member of his flock. They had just turned to a hillside road overlooking a lake, when to his utter amazement he beheld right down there below him a group of his own people happily engaged in curling. So shocked was the minister at the sight of such appalling wickedness that for a brief spell he sat there gazing, until his painful reverie was suddenly broken in upon by his companion, the elder, who during these same brief moments had been, not shocked, but angry at the sluggish sweeping of his fellow elder, Jock Anderson. Completely forgetting whom he was with, he shouted down: "Wot the de'il's ailin' ye, Jock Anderson? Move, dom ye, move! Soup 'er up soup 'er up!" Recovering himself, and thoroughly ashamed, now, he faced his old pastor and guide in fear and trembling. Yet, logically defending himself, he broke out: "Ah, my auld meenister, ye dinna ken, ye couldna ken, and dom it, mon, ye'll never ken thot I jus couldna help mysel', for yon's a fearfu' game."

Taking up again the brief list of references to curling personnel of the seventeenth century we find the name of a covenanting minister, William Guthrie. He is reported, quite truthfully, to have been far more liberal-minded than his reverend brethren, seeing that he enjoyed all the health-giving recreations which then prevailed, such as fishing, fowling and playing on the ice. A tribute to him reads: "Let his memory live for ever among us, for a worthier than he never lifted the channel-stane."

The next reference to that period gives us a glimpse of some lairds enjoying a game of curling in the border district. One of the players, Sir William Scot of Harden, was in danger of being taken by forces sent expressly for such a purpose (he seems to have been a supporter of the Earl of Argyle in his rebellion against Charles II) but he was warned and fled the game in time. However, he was later taken to Edinburgh and put in irons because he refused to give the name of the man who warned him!

The revolution of 1688, to which all the troubles of the century had led, brought about the inauguration of a new and brighter era for both curlers and non-curlers. On this matter Dr. Kerr said:

> Those ancient worthies, who in the dark days cultivated the curling art under difficulties now unknown to us—and who faithfully upheld the cause of curling till the day of freedom, peace and brotherhood saw its recognition as a national game—will ever deserve honour from succeeding generations of curlers.

A final seventeenth century reference to curling is found in a rare work written by a James Wallace, then minister of Kirkwell, which ran as follows:

> To the East of the Mainland lyes Copinsha, a little isle but very conspicuous to seamen, in which and in severell other

places in this Countrey are to be found in great plentie excellent stones for the game called Curling.

And of curling in the eighteenth century, our chief authority, Dr. Kerr, said:

> Between 1700 and 1800 the literary references to curling show that it was generally practised in Scotland. Several accounts of the game and of interesting bonspiels are given; curling societies are formed; and curling is by the end of the century entitled to be regarded as the great national winter game.

Also, referring back to the eighteenth century, Ramsay said, in 1811:

> At Edinburgh, where curlers are collected from all the counties of Scotland, this amusement has been long enjoyed. And in so great a repute was it toward the beginning of the last century, that the magistrates are said to have gone to it and returned in a body, with a band of music before them, playing tunes adapted to the occasion. Then it was practised chiefly on the North Loch, before it was drained, and at Canonmills.

There is an interesting reference to curling in Sir Walter Scott's *Guy Mannering*:

> On the frozen bosom of the lake itself were a multitude of moving figures, some flitting along with the velocity of swallows, some sweeping in the most graceful circles and others deeply interested in a less active pastime, crowding around the spot where the inhabitants of two rival parishes contended for the prize at curling,—an honour of no small importance if we were to judge from the anxiety expressed both by the players and the bystanders.

# CHAPTER III

# FORMATION OF CLUBS OR SOCIETIES---
# A READING OF OLD MINUTE-BOOKS

*Curlers at annual meets in ardent throngs*
*Were wont at times to rant or sing like linnets,*
*Until the chairman stopped their boasts and songs*
*To hear the usual reading of the Minutes.*

THE FORMATION OF CURLING CLUBS—OR SOCIETIES AS THEY
were also called—showed from the beginning, on the part of
their Scottish founders, a general determination to instil and
then maintain, as high a standard of conduct among the individual members as possible. This common desire for order
and decency both in action and speech was approved, in
principle, by all. But unfortunately each parish had its own
set of rules and regulations and was wont to comply only
with what suited itself.

As an outstanding example of these differences in
method of play we cite a case in which players, accustomed
to using heavy stones on a 30-yard rink, were matched against
an equal number of players using much lighter stones and
accustomed to a rink of 40 yards. The reader—if a curler—
needs only a moment to see that the result would almost
certainly be determined by the rink's length. To the uninitiated I would explain that if the game were played on the
shorter rink it would be an easy task for the heavier armed
men to get their great stones up to the tee from which, on
account of their immense weight, it would be difficult for

40

them to be removed, almost impossible if well guarded; while on the longer rink the tee would be out of range to the heavy stones and the lighter-armed men would have it all their own way. In fact, curling history gives us an apt instance in which a rink made up of lighter-stone men about to play on a 30-yard ice sheet suddenly refused point blank to start the game on seeing one of their opponents equipped with a cobbler's heavy lapstone. Under such conditions one can readily believe that even in those early times many a curler looked ahead to a day when rinks would be of a standard length and stones of a standard weight and shape.

Tradition has it that at both Lochleven and Linlithgow such organizations as curling clubs had existed from time immemorial. A committee of the Kinross Club after careful investigation came to the decision that there were good grounds for claiming the existence of a curling club at Lochleven as far back as 1668. The time of the founding of the Linlithgow Curling Club cannot, however, be stated with any degree of accuracy. The earliest reference to the Linlithgow Curling Club occurs in the minutes of the Dunfermline Club of 2nd February 1792:

"Mr. John Gibson, a visiting brother from Linlithgow Club."

Curling, therefore, must have been carried on in a more or less spasmodic manner for well over a century before the growing need of a more orderly procedure practically forced these clubs into existence. Also, in those same clubless years, curling, in some few localities, appears—after having come into existence—to have suddenly ceased functioning for some now unknown reason. As an example one might cite the incident of the centenarian who stated that in his opinion curling had never been played at any time near his neighbourhood — even though some old-time curling stones found at the bottom of a recently drained loch proved him to have been wrong. His error, however, is quite explainable as curling stones were often left out on the ice after a game and a sudden change of weather caused them to break through the weakened ice and become lost beyond recovery. As a result the game itself frequently became lost for long periods of time. As substantiating this, curling history records that many old-time curling stones have, after long years of submersion, been found during operations carried out with the purpose of making certain tarns and ponds safer for curling.

Consequently it should not be considered unreasonable to suppose that curlers in a number of Scottish parishes may in times gone by have been forced—through such accidental losses of stones—to forego for indefinite periods the pleasures of the game. Of all this, however, no one can speak positively since there were no curling records in pre-club times.

Once curling clubs came into existence, due in all likelihood to the necessity of arranging matches with outside parishes in a standard manner, the game's future was assured. The coming of clubs raised the dignity of curling. Under the control of these societies curling was for the first time given an authoritative voice where one duly appointed man spoke, not for himself, but for the club he represented. It was, in fine, a splendid forward and upward move; and once a few such organizations had set the example, other curling districts were, as the subsequent history of the game has shown, certain to follow.

By the close of the eighteenth century there were twenty-eight curling clubs or societies affiliated with the Royal Caledonian Curling Club, as well as fourteen not affiliated. The first was the Kilsyth Club of Stirling, formed in 1716, and the latest the Dundee Club, formed in 1800. Unfortunately only a few of these forty-two clubs preserved any records of their early activities.

The records of the Muthill Club of Perth, a club founded

in 1739, antedate those of all other clubs in Scotland. The following rules and statutes, moved and approved by the charter members of that old Muthill, should—to a curler—repay a reading:

1. That each member shall attend the Precess of any quorum of the Society when called, unless they have a reasonable excuse, under the penalty of Six Shillings Scots.
2. That no match of curling shall be taken up with another Parish until five of the members of the Society be previously acquainted therewith, and those that shall be chosen to play in any such match are not to absent themselves therefrom, under penalty of Five Shillings Sterling, and being extruded the Society till payment.
3. That the annual election of all officers of the Society shall be upon the first Tuesday of ————————.
4. That there shall be no wagers, cursing or swearing, during the time of game under the penalty of Two Shillings Scots for each oath, and the fines for by wagers to be at the discretion of the Precess and the other members present, and the wagers in themselves to be void and null.
5. That every residing member of the Society betwixt now and the next annual election shall provide himself in a curling stone, to be kept in this place under the penalty of one Shilling Sterling.
6. That all the money received by the Society for the entry of new members or Fynes be kept for the use of the Society in general.
7. That every member shall pay yearly to the Treasurer Four Shillings Scots, for the use aforesaid.
8. That after this date at taking up any matches betwixt any two parties they are only to have choice about.
9. That there shall be no additions or alterations made of the above rules but at the yearly meetings.

And it is recommended to the Society in general to provide four right leading stones to be equally divided in all matches, etc., and the Committee to draw up the men for the match.

Of Muthill's method of play, except for what may be assumed from the fact that only one stone was played per man, little is known. With one stone per man, however, it could be assumed that seven or more players per side was the usual procedure. At these old club meetings nothing seemed too trivial to record. For instance, under date February 7, 1789, the Muthill Club preserved this entry in its records: "To Isabel White for whiskey for cleaning the ice, £0.1s.3d."

The minutes do not state how the whiskey was to be applied!

The type of stones used by members of this club in the days of its beginnings were probably those of the "Bible" and the "Goose". (Figures 18 and 19, Page 74).

The records of the Sanquhar Club, founded in 1774, extended through a century of time. Two of the entries recall Statute 4 of the Muthill Club:

Jan'y 1782

Walter M'Turk, Surgeon, was expelled the Society for offering a gross insult in calling them a parcel of d———d scoundrels.

17th Dec. 1788

The meeting proceeded to chuse officers for the ensuing year when Mr. Walter M'Turk, Surgeon, was chosen Preses.

Between sometime in January 1782 and December 1788, the surgeon, apparently, had changed his ways!

The rules of St. Bride's Club of Douglas were similar to those of Muthill, yet the two here given will be of interest:

Rule 4. The players shall be divided by the office bearers into racks and placed in those racks (rinks) in all parish games, and any person refusing to play in the place allotted to him shall be fined in the sum of sixpence.

Rule 6. Any person refusing to play a parish game, when warned by the officer (unless he can give such an excuse as the majority of his rack shall approve of) shall be fined in the sum of one Shilling.

The Jubilee Celebration of St. Bride's was held in 1842; and from a poem recited on the occasion anent the curling of Bailie Hamilton, we read:

*The rink in length was forty yards and nine*
*As measured by Tom Haddow with his line.*

The most outstanding of all Scotland's curling clubs, The Duddingston, named from the small loch at the foot of Arthur's Seat, was founded in 1795 and after it had enjoyed thirty years of existence, Dr. Cairnie, the first R.C.C.C. President, had this to say in its favour:

> In mentioning Societies of Curlers, the Duddingston certainly merits to be placed first in the list as containing many members who are highly eminent for scientific knowledge, wealth, respectability and worth.

It can further be said that the Duddingston Club justly ranks as the one most entitled to the honour of being regarded as the chief forerunner of the Grand Caledonian Curling Club of 1838. Its members, being nearly all drawn from Edinburgh, doubtless were eager to learn new methods in curling.

The Resolutions and Rules, as framed and upheld by the Duddingston Club, plainly reveal both as to number and kind the disputes and kindred worries to be looked for in nearly all keenly matched games. To begin with their resolutions:

1. Resolved that the sole object of this institution is the enjoyment of the game of curling, which, while it adds vigour to the body, contributes to vivacity of mind and the promotion of the social and generous feelings.

2. Resolved that peace and unanimity, the great ornaments of society, shall reign among them, and that virtue, without which no accomplishment is truly valuable and no enjoyment really satisfactory, shall be the aim of all their actions.

3. Resolved that to be virtuous is to reverence our God, religion, laws and king, and they hereby declare their reverence for and attachment to the same.

As for the rules, the Committee responsible declared, in presenting them for acceptance, that:

They' (the rules) had been prepared with the greatest care, most of which are strictly observed in those counties in which the game of curling prevails.

### Rules in Curling to be Observed by the Duddingston Curling Society:

1. The usual length of a rink is from thirty-six to forty-four yards inclusive; but this will be regulated by circumstances and the agreement of parties. When a game is begun the rink is not to be changed or altered, unless by the consent of the majority of the players; nor is it to be shortened, unless it clearly appears that the majority are unable to make up.

2. The hog score to be one-sixth part of the length of the rink distant from the tee, and every stone to be deemed a hog the sole of which does not clear the score.

3. Each player to foot in such a manner that in delivering his stone, he brings it over the tee.

4. The order of play adopted at the beginning must be observed during the whole course of a game.

5. All curling stones to be of a CIRCULAR shape. No stone is to be changed throughout a game unless it happens to be broken; and the largest fragment of such stone to count, without any necessity of playing with it more. If a stone rolls or is upset, it must be placed upon its sole where it stops. Should the handle quit a stone in the delivery, the player must keep hold of it, otherwise he will not be entitled to replay the shot.

6. A player may sweep his own stone the whole length of the rink; his party not to sweep until it has passed the hog score at the farther end, and his adversaries not to sweep until it has passed the tee, the sweeping to be always to a side.

7. None of the players on any occasion, to cross or go upon the middle of the rink.

8. If in sweeping or otherwise a running stone is marred by any of the party to which it belongs, it must be put off the ice; if by any of the adverse party, it must be placed agreeable to the direction which was given to the player; and if it is marred by any other means, the player may take his

shot again. Should a stone at rest be accidentally displaced, it must be put as nearly as possible in its former situation.

9. Every player is to be ready when his turn comes, and to take no more than a reasonable time to play his shot. Should he, by mistake, play with a wrong stone, it must be replaced where it stops by the one with which he ought to have played.

10. A doubtful shot is to be measured by some neutral person, whose determination shall be final.

11. Before beginning to play, each party must name one of their number for directing their game. The players of his party may give their advice to the one so named, but they cannot control his direction, nor are they to address themselves to the person who is about to play. Each director when it is his turn to play, to name one of his party to take the charge for him. Every player to follow the direction given to him.

12. Should any question arise the determination of which may not be provided for by the words and spirit of the rules now established, each party to choose one of their number in order to determine it. If the two so chosen differ in opinion, they are to name an umpire whose decision shall be final.

Such were Duddingston's rules and regulations governing the game of curling. They were framed and approved and brought into operation in the year 1806. Three years later, 1809, the Duddingston curlers established Point Competitions, a phase of the game utterly unknown in Eighteenth century curling. A gold medal, properly inscribed and embellished, was requested and granted. The winner was "to have his success announced in the newspapers and to be allowed, if he should so choose, to append a small badge to his medal, expressive of his having been victor for the year."

Only three points, however, were thought worthy of being played—viz: DRAWING, STRIKING and INWICK-ING—at each of which the competitors were allowed four chances. "Point medal" playing grew to be so popular with the curlers that one Sir Alexander Boswell of Auchinlech penned a poem, the three verses of which indicate the great interest taken in this annual Battle of the Points:

*Let lads dam the waters in ilka how trough,*
*For cheerin' frost comes wi' December;*
*And curlers o' Scotland on Duddingston Loch*
*The glorious medal remember.*

Chorus: *Duddingston Loch*
*Duddingston Loch*
*Strain ilka nerve, shouther, back-bane and hough.*

*Let rogues and let fools rin to cards and to dice,*
*And gamblin', sit girnin' and gurlin';*
*But honest men ken that tho' slipp'ry the ice,*
*Still fair play and fun gang wi' curlin'.*

Chorus:

*Then ring it round Reekie, our auld bizzin' byke,*
*That the rinks are a' measured and soupit;*
*And out flee the lads, to draw, inwick and strike,*
*Frae plough, counter, desk, bar and pu'pit.*

Chorus:

The Three Duddingston Resolutions should stand approved for all time, whereas the Rules could only survive if they made provision for every possible contingency. Neither must it be overlooked that those twelve rules applied only to the Duddingston Club and not to the slowly increasing number of similar organizations outside the Edinburgh pale. And there must have been quite a number in 1806 whose members were far from being ready to adopt either a standard measurement for rinks, a standard shape for stones, or a standard number of players a side.

Thus the Duddingston code of rules, although an effort in the right direction and fully deserving the praise it then received, was not the ultimate goal that had to be attained if curling were ever to become both a standard and a national game.

All this can perhaps be better understood after we have noted the few differing methods of play still prevailing among some of Duddingston's curling contemporaries.

The curlers of Hamilton had long been accustomed to play seven, sometimes eight men a side, and up to 1836, two years before the founding of the Royal Club, one stone per man was the rule; and in delivering the stone they never used the hack, but each player braced himself by a "crisp" or "tricker" which gripped the ice.

A visitor to Scotland in 1772 related that in his time the rink, or distance from tee to tee, was not generally more than 30 yards; that the players steadied themselves by means of crampits, in appearance like stirrup-irons, and fixed to the shoes like skates; and that in a contest there were usually eight on a side with each playing one stone.

Contrast these 30 yard rinks with the 49 yard rink that was measured by Tom Haddow with his line! The players in those old 30 yard rinks were probably using something like the "Soo" or the great "Jubilee" type of stones (see Figures 10 and 18, Pages 72 and 74), and the coming in of the longer rinks would have put them practically out of business.

Yet for years those same swashbucklers with their heavy boulders had been wont to smash the lighter channel-stones to an extent, as was said, that would have furnished road metal sufficient to cover a few Scottish miles. Naturally this marksmanship style of play with its damaging results gained for these curling sharpshooters the loud applause of admiring bystanders.

Dr. Kerr points out that although in the early nineteenth century there was much progress and enthusiasm in the matter of curling in Scotland, and that "in most parishes the curling club became a recognized necessity", there was, also, much confusion. Curlers being conservative, the advanced methods and rules of Duddingston were "only slowly adopted".

Yet, only in two points were the Duddingston rule framers decidedly at variance with most other curling groups: in Rule I, in which the allowable rink lengths may vary from 36 to 42 yards, thus barring the 30 yard rinks at Duddingston Loch; and in Rule 5 which stated that only circular stones should be allowed in play, thus forbidding the ice to the multiform boulders that generally went with the 30-yard rinks.

These were friendly points of difference, and it was not until the Duddingston rules had been revised and incorporated with those of the R. C. C. that we find curling standardized as to the number of men allowed per side and the number of stones allotted per man. All these gradual approaches towards a general uniformity were inevitable if the game were to survive as a national sport.

CHAPTER IV

# THE FORMATION OF THE ROYAL CALEDONIAN CURLING CLUB

*Curling, Auld Scotia's pride, her wondrous game,*
*Beloved by all who in her councils con*
*Such laws and rules as may exalt her fame*
*And justify that world resounding name——*
*"The Royal Curling Club of Caledon"!*

THE PROGRESS OF CURLING IMMEDIATELY PRECEDING THE FOR-
mation of the Grand Caledonian Curling Club in 1838 was
not seriously impeded by the social and political upheavals
occurring throughout the British Isles. Indeed the only ob-
stacle to the union that finally took place was the reluctance
on the part of many curlers throughout Scotland to agree to
the adoption of a uniform style of play, and so become on all
sides, true "brithers" of the stone and broom. Not withstand-
ing this reluctance in almost every parish in which curling
was played, the idea of the formation of one Grand Curling
Organization was steadily gaining in favour.

One might have expected that uniformity in methods of
play would need only to be suggested to be generally adopted. Facts tell us that throughout the years covered in the
preceding chapter curling clubs kept on making and abiding
by their own rules. The Duddingston twelve commandments
were, with perhaps a few exceptions, left to Duddingston.
The rules which permitted one stone per man and the use
of ice-mangling crampits and trickers were approved by the

51

majority of parish clubs, probably because the prevailing thinness of the ice on the curling ponds barred the deep cutting of hacks. The committees of some clubs not only approved of one stone per man but in a few extreme cases had allowed the number of players a side to range from four to five times four. On many occasions this utter lack of uniformity led to heated arguments and grudging concessions before a match could begin.

Ever on the side of peace and progress was one of curling's immortals, John Cairnie, who through all his adult years never for a day lost faith in the coming of the new era in which all curlers would be "brithers" in a saner way—the way of complete uniformity in methods of play. Indeed, from all we have read of him John Cairnie must have been a truly great man.

A brief glance at the state of affairs in some of the better known centres of curling will give us a general idea of the game's various ups and downs. At Greenoch "a flourishing club existed", while in Paisley the game was going strong, apparently, for John Good (Johnny Gude), weaver, had supplied the curlers with 200 pairs of stones! A club there, whose members "went into the game scientifically", had ten rinks of seven players each.

In the county of Lanark although the list of clubs was small for its population, the curling strongholds of Douglas, Lesmahagow, Cambusnethan and Hamilton still existed and "manfully upheld the cause". At Hamilton, for instance, an advanced type of stone seemed to have been used as far back as the Hamilton v. Garthland bonspiel in 1784. Here the hollowed bottom, now so common in Canada, was introduced, while at Wishaw they tried a peculiar type of stone, one sole of which ran on three projecting points, and the other on a circle of about one inch. Some of the stones had steel bottoms, while others were cast-iron with bottoms of steel or brass. Concerning these fearsome types, the poet of the Bathgate Club wrote as follows of the consternation among his fellow members at having to play against opponents so well armed:

> *Before the icy war began*
> *Our hearts had well nigh failed us*
> *As we surveyed their famous stanes*
> *Prepared to assail us.*
>
> *For some were big as ony cheese*
> *And some had bright steel bottoms,*
> *Some ran on feet, some ran on nane;*
> *Ours looked like bits o' totums.*

Many clubs in and around Glasgow carried on the game. The Anderston Club, one of the oldest was formed "for the healthful, cheering amusement of curling; no cursing or swearing was allowed, and the club required of all the members polite, kindly behaviour as brothers."

One of these western clubs, the Willowbank, constructed a pond at a cost of £287, according to the records of the club, while in Dumbarton the Kirkintilloch Club united "lairds, farmers, shopkeepers and wabsters, at the roaring game."

In the more southern districts we have the curling club of Dumfries, one of whose rules, not an altogether progressive one, was that the mode of play in the choice of skips and other matters respecting the game, be settled by the majority of those present at the ice board at commencing of play. On the other hand this club started a curling magazine and, although the first issue was the last, yet in itself it was a praiseworthy move.

The Lochmaben Club had a set of rules which were partly rewritten by the indefatigable Sir Richard Broun, who based his alterations on those of Duddingston. Duddingston itself, by precept and example established the way to more scientific curling. In fact it cannot be too often repeated that

Duddingston contributed more than any other club to the transition of curling from the old ways to the new.

In the more northern group of clubs, Stirling County all through this period kept herself sufficiently in the limelight to let her neighbours know that she favoured a gradual improvement in methods of curling.

At Dunfermline, Markinch, Leven and Kilconquhar, curling was then so popular that at the last-named club it was no rare occurrence for the players, after curling a whole day, to retire at twilight for a little refreshment before resuming the game, not by the light of the moon, but by lantern-light, keeping it up till cock-crow!

Both the Doune and the Ardoch clubs, although enthusiastic and vigorous, were slow in the matter of progress, for, up to 1828, they both used the old type of stone, with one allowed to each man, and nine men a side. They also stayed with the 30 yard rink. Indicative, surely, of the hasty tempers of the members was the set of rules laid down for observance, as follows:

1. Only one member shall speak at a time and in addressing the president the speaker shall arise to his feet.

2. Whiskey punch to be the usual drink of the club in order to encourage the growth of barley.

3. NO POLITICS OF CHURCH OR STATE TO BE DIS-CUSSED.

4. No member to speak of the faults of another member in curling, nor deride the office-bearers, nor dis-obey the orders of the day.

5. Any member convicted of robbery or reset of theft shall have his name erased from the roll of members.

6. Any member appearing at a meeting the worse of liquor shall be obliged to leave immediately for the day.

7. Any member who swears, dictates to another how to vote, or persists in trifling motions without being supported shall be fined.

8. The amount of each fine is to be 6d.

The ancient club of Muthill was, in this same period, both friendly and to the fore; but curling news from Perth was somewhat vague. Better news, however, and a brighter side of the ledger, was evident in the progressive spirit shown by the Clunie Club where the Duddingston rules were slowly coming into favour due largely to the missionary work of Principal Baird of Edinburgh University. Dr. Baird, in his younger days, had been settled as a minister at Dunkeld, the home of the Clunie Club, and after his departure had continued through letters his intimate friendship with its curlers.

Farther north, the Duke of Athole's interest is indicated in the following note by Sir Richard Broun in 1830:

> The late Duke of Athole suggested a new mode of curling, viz., upon skates and with long poles forked at the end. The player fixes this upon the handle of the stone and then retires ten or twelve yards from the tee. He next swiftly pushes it forward, humouring its motion, and having his eye fixed on the object to be aimed for at the farther end; when the stone reaches the tee he gives it the requisite impulse. This is described as an elegant mode and makes a highly interesting game.

It is interesting to note that Dr. Kerr thought that the bent-down handles on many of the old stones that he had seen indicated that the Duke's plan had been tried in a good many places, and more especially with the old implements that were at the time falling into disuse.

In the eastern areas the game, up to this time, had many enthusiasts, but they appear to have been concentrated in fewer clubs. In Edinburgh, of course, the national game had always been "recognized and encouraged in a manner worthy of the Scottish capital." The magistrates would grace the annual opening of the winter sport on the Nor' Loch, while the clubs at nearby Canonmills and Duddingston had as members many of Edinburgh's distinguished citizens, too. The Rosslyn Club, along with the Penicuick Club, gained

particular distinction in a great bonspiel between Midlothian
and the Upper Ward of Lanarkshire in 1831, played on
Slipperfield Loch, Peeblesshire. The minutes of the former
contained a testimony to such matches "as they tend to
strengthen the rivalry which is peculiar to the game, promote
dexterity in the art, and enlarge the sphere of social intercourse by bringing together kindred spirits that but for such
occasions would never meet."

In the County of Peebles a club was in existence at the
county town in 1821. Here, at a meeting December 24, a
Mr. James Turnbull laid before the members a set of regulations which included one that said "every member shall
be able to prove himself the lawful owner of at least one
stone", another that said, "when ladies come near the rink
and are disposed to play, the skips shall have the privilege
of instructing them to handle the stones agreeable to the
rules of the game", and a third, as follows: "when a member
falls and is hurt, the rest shall not laugh, but render him
every assistance to enable him to regain his former erect
position."

Over in the county of Selkirk, the Ettrick Curling Club
was presided over by the Ettrick Shepherd himself, James
Hogg, who was "as devoted to the channel-stane as he was
to the fiddle." Then in Berwick, in 1822, the enthusiastic
members of the Duns Club are recorded as agreeing to drink
the health of one William Hay of Drummelzier at every
meeting of the club "for indulging it with the use of Hen-poo
Pond." These same members, apparently, associated their
curling luck with their clothes, for Dr. Kerr found in the club
records that one club match was lost because one of the
players "wore a pea-jacket", and another because one of the
losers "wore a great-coat".

Curling Clubs at Kelso and Jedburgh, county of Rox-
burgh, are recorded as being established near the end of the
eighteenth century. Although details of the Jedburgh club

activities are rather meagre, it is known that teams played for beef and greens or "a mutchkin of toddy", and also bet some "dross" on their matches!

Dr. Kerr, in summing up his survey of curling in Scotland during the period 1800-1838, wrote as follows:

> It appears that the game was most popular in the counties of the western and southern district—such as Ayr, Renfrew, Lanark, Dumfries and Kirkcudbright. In the eastern counties—such as Haddington, Berwick and Roxburgh—it had not yet made great progress. In such counties as Edinburgh, Fife, Kinross and Perth, we hear of many notable clubs and players at this time; but among the people generally the game cannot be said to have been so popular as in the counties we have mentioned. Beyond Perth and Forfar curling appears to have been at this time little known. Its benign influence had not extended to the Highlands.

The year 1838 saw the founding of the Grand Caledonian Curling Club on July 25, with its headquarters in the Scottish capital, and having for its object "the regulation of the laws and methods of curling by the united deliberations of representatives from all the clubs of the country." This is considered the most important and far-reaching event in the whole history of curling. Its first president was John Cairnie, the man who had so long and so effectively worked to make that founding an accomplished fact.

The establishing of a Supreme Court of Curling had been suggested previously by Sir Richard Broun. In defence of Sir Richard's suggestion John Cairnie wrote in 1833:

> The author of the *Mem. Cur.* has suggested to us a scheme for the formation of An Amateur Curling Club for Scotland, and we trust he will soon, in a second edition of his work, furnish the curlers of this country with the particulars. He has been so kind as to suggest to us some of the items connected with the plan of formation; and we sincerely wish the talented gentleman's views of the subject may be realized. We think it would be a very desirable matter that, connected with this curling club, it should be recommended that every curling society in Scotland should correspond, and give in a list of

their office-bearers, the number of curlers, matches played and any matter connected with the game that is interesting.

Sir Richard failed to carry out the suggested plan at the time expected; but later in 1834 the St. Bride's (of Douglas) Curling Society at one of its meetings received from a Captain Paterson the news that the new edition of Broun's work had at last been issued and contained the following:

## PROSPECTUS

Amateur Curling Club of Scotland
Instituted 1834
For Promoting and Cherishing the Noble and National
Game of Curling

Resolution,—That the Amateur Curling Club shall be entirely exclusive, embracing the names of such curlers alone as are entitled to be handed down to posterity as associated par excellence with the ice of the nineteenth century. Members shall be admitted——

(1) Ex-officio,—From being presidents or office-bearers of any curling society throughout Scotland.

(2) Ex-merito,—From being distingué either from literary production upon the subject of curling or from inventions of some kind practically connected with the game.

(3) Ex-suffragio,—From very high scientific skill; gaining a medal or a recommendation from the office-bearers of the local society to which the candidate belongs, shall be necessary for admission under this head.

In 1809 when Sir Alexander Boswell wrote the verses on playing of points he certainly gave to all and sundry the distinct impression that at Duddingston Loch—when the ice was "a' measured and soupit"—among those fleeing to take part in the competitions were ploughmen, shopmen and others of that ilk. But in this curling prospectus of a quarter of a century later those same sons of toil would seem to have all migrated to another planet. For example in Resolution 2, the word *distingué*, assumes the place of the natural and better word, "distinguished". This little break into French could of course have been ignored; but when *les distingués* was translated to mean that the proposed Amateur Club was to be under the distinguished patronage of two dukes, and that two more dukes in addition to three lords and an earl were suggested as choices for presidents, and two baronets for vice-presidents, the wonder is that the prospectus ever secured a hearing. Dr. Kerr referred to it as "a mutual admiration society" and reported that "as might be expected, it came to nothing."

In 1838 we have a Dr. Arnott, in his *Laws of Curling* emphasizing the crying need of uniform methods of play along with the additional need of knowing all the initiatory words and signs which tend to bind curlers into one brotherhood:

> All brothers have probably the same *grip*; but there appears to be considerable variation as to the *word*. This last is to be regretted and might easily be remedied by a convention formed of the Secretaries or some accredited office-bearers of the principal initiated clubs of Scotland.

Following this practical suggestion an unsigned notice appeared on 26th May 1838, in the *North British Advertiser* urging that a Curling Meeting be held on 20th June at the Waterloo Hotel in Edinburgh, at 11 a.m.

> For the purpose of making the mysteries more uniform in future, and, if requisite, to form a grand court to which all provincial ones shall be subject, and to elect a grand president, with other office bearers. It is hoped that all Brethren who see this notice will direct the attention of their President or Secretary to it without delay. 16th May 1838.

The notice accomplished the purpose its unknown author intended. On that 20th day of June at 11 a.m. a small group of curlers met at the Waterloo Hotel and having waited overtime for the unknown adviser to show himself in person, were on the point of departing, a little bewildered, when a gentleman appeared at the door. With all the appearance of one expected, he presented his card: "John Cairnie of Curling Hall, Largs."

It took only a few minutes to assure the small group of assembled curlers that the right man had appeared at the right time. His pleasing yet dominant personality so impressed the now enthusiastic group that he was unanimously appointed chairman. He called the meeting to order at once, and although the meeting was small, and brief, it accomplished important business. A properly signed notice was at once sent to the *North British Advertiser*:

> To Curlers—In consequence of an advertisement which appeared in the North British Advertiser of 26th May 1838, a MEETING of CURLERS was held in the Waterloo Hotel on the 20th inst., John Cairnie Esq., of Curling Hall, Largs, in the chair. Deputations from various clubs appeared, who approved generally of adopting a uniform set of regulations applicable to the whole of Scotland, assimilating the technical terms, forming a Court of Reference, etc. But anxious for a fuller representation of the different clubs throughout the country in order to perpetuate and connect more closely the Brotherhood in this Ancient National Game, they adjourned to Wednesday, 25th July next, at 12 o'clock, in the Waterloo Hotel when they hope the different clubs of Scotland will make a point of sending deputations.
>
> John Cairnie, Chairman.

The meeting of 25th July turned out to be a representative one, consisting of forty-four men backed by thirty-six clubs connected with districts from Dumfries to Perth and from the Forth to the Clyde. Then and there in that large Assembly Room the G.C.C.C. (afterwards R.C.C.C.) was born and its coming into the world was made the occasion for enthusiastic acclaim. Without any undue delay it was formally proposed and unanimously passed: "That this meeting do form itself into a club composed of the different initiated clubs of Scotland under the name of 'The Grand Caledonian Curling Club'."

Dr. John Cairnie, with no other name even suggested, was made the Club's first president, and after the meeting had closed, the members all sat down to a genuine curlers' dinner.

In the selection of a managing committee the Duddingston Club was accorded a special honour in having all three of its delegates included. The drafting of the Grand Club's initial Constitution was, in the main, done by another great figure in the curling life of Scotland, Captain James Dalgleish, a man concerning whose death at a later day the Royal Club's committee thus gave expression to the general opinion: "Gentlemanly, genial and hearty in manner, a good curler and a grand skip. We feel as curlers that we have lost one of the best of friends."

The Grand Club experienced a piece of good fortune four years after its founding when the Queen and her Consort, Prince Albert, paid a visit to Scotland in 1842. The Club's officials made the Royal visit an occasion for presenting the Prince with a pair of curling stones with the expressed desire that the new organization be given the favourable notice of His Royal Highness. At the same time the Prince gave his cordial assent to the suggestion that he become the club's patron. Nor was it long after this visit before permission was formally granted that the word "Royal" be added to the club names already in use. But when the word "Royal" was added, the word "Grand" appeared to have become more or less superfluous and hence was allowed to drop with the result that the name finally became, "The Royal Caledonian Curling Club".

On the death of the Prince Consort, His Royal Highness, Albert Edward, Prince of Wales, consented to take his father's place as the club's patron.

Both the work and the influence of this fine organization

will in all likelihood increase in view of the corresponding increase of clubs in Auld Scotia hersel' and in England to say naught of unnumbered thousands of curlers from Ontario to the Pacific Coast and with many additional thousands from Quebec to the Eastern Maritimes, including Newfoundland.

There remain, in addition to all these, our brithers o' the broom in the United States, counting those whose clubs are affiliated with the Grand National Curling Club of America as well as a goodly number of clubs from Detroit, west. On the front of the cover of every *Annual* published by the American G. N. C. C., these old familiar words stand out in the plainest of print: "We're Brithers A'."

Considering, therefore, this wonderful spread of the game from Scotland over so great a portion of the globe even including Norway, Switzerland, Sweden and New Zealand, and considering also whence came those auld, auld words, "We're Brithers A' ", no curler—dwell where he may— should ever allow himself to forget that Scotland is the beloved motherland of the game.

For generations her curlers have shown both by precept and by example what is meant by the "Democracy of Curling". In the varied ranks of her players, nobles, professional men, merchants, shepherds, cottars and ploughmen stand side by side. Still together do they sit down to enjoy their annual beef and greens. We are told that the genial Duke of Athole, on the night of the grand match at Linlithgow in 1848, had 170 brother curlers around him at a dinner held at the Star and Garter. And on a similar occasion at Kilmarnock in 1841, Lord Eglinton, long a keen curler, thus replied to a toast to his health:

> I have the earnest wish to encourage the game and sports of my native country, and more especially such games and sports as by their nature are open alike to poor and rich. Among these I am sure there is none that can be compared to curling.

In conclusion we quote some words spoken by the venerable John Cairnie at that same meeting, in reply to the kind words spoken of him:

> I am now an old curler, and very unable to speak as I should like; but I am a keen curler; the spirit is willing but the flesh is weak. I think I shall curl to the last.

It was the old hero's farewell, Dr. Kerr related. A year thereafter he played his last stone and "quitted the rink of life, curling to the last, as he thought he should."

# CHAPTER V

# CURLING EQUIPMENT OF LONG AGO

*It boots not whence the curler hails,*
*If curler keen an' staunch he be,*
*Frae Scotland, England, Ireland, Wales,*
*Or ither land ayont the sea;*
*A social britherhood are we,*
*And after we are deid an' gane*
*We'll live in literature an' lair*
*In annals o' the channel-stane.*

MORE THAN FOUR CENTURIES WERE NEEDED FOR THE DEVELOPment of the highly polished and symmetrically finished stone now used by the curling brotherhood of the world. During this period three distinct types of stones have successively come into existence—the third being the one in use to-day.

First we have the *kuting* type, with holes and hollows cut on opposite sides of the stone, made for the insertion of the thumb and the fingers respectively; the second type was an appropriately shaped river-bed stone, roughly hewn, and crudely equipped with a smith-made iron handle and called by the general name of "channel-stone"; the third type is the round or circular stone that from a rude beginning, by slow degrees evolved into the almost perfect instrument which curlers enjoy to-day.

There was, also, a very primitive type of stone, known as the *loofie*. But from what we have been able to discover, the *loofie* game was little other than quoit pitching trans-

64

ferred from the land to the ice. The *loofie* stones were flat, being described in Jamieson's Scottish dictionary as being somewhat the shape and size of a man's hand—from the old Scottish term, *loof*, a hand. They are said to have been given a long swinging throw toward a mark, the player trusting the remainder of its course to the smoothness of the ice. To our way of thinking, however, it could hardly be called curling, though it probably pointed the way.

The *kuting* stone was swung from behind and sent toward a mark by a curving sweep, meeting the ice at as fine or "well floored" an angle as possible, thus giving it the maximum chance for a smooth run, somewhat as was done with the *loofie*. It was far from being a heavy stone and the reason is easy to understand when we consider that the only workable grips lay in the two cuttings—one on the upper and one on the lower side. The stone, therefore, with only the thumb and fingers to manage it, had to be light. Their weights, it is recorded, varied from 5 pounds to 25 or 26 pounds. Yet, light and faulty as they were, they continued to be the corner stones of curling for a century and a half before they were driven off the ice by something better. That they had fallen from grace can be gleaned from the old Scottish rhymes. The poet, James Hogg, a contemporary of Scott, and already known to us as the *Ettrick Shepherd*, thus contrasts the earlier *kutings* with the handle-equipped channel-stones which finally replaced them:

> I've played at quoiting in my day,
> And maybe I may do't again;
> But still unto myself I say
> This is no the channel-stane.

A second curling poet, Walter Watson, writes of the *quoiting* stone in the following rather jolly strain:

> The loch's aye the loch whaur in cauld days o'yore
> The lee-side was cheered by the quoitin-stane's roar,
> Whaur aft our auld daddies wud off wi' their pladdies
> As they had been shown by their daddies afore.

As to the words *quoiting, kuting* and *coiting*, it should be remembered that for a long time they were used to describe one game, and may have continued to be so used in a few parts of Scotland well on into the second period when the handle-equipped stones were dominant. Sir Richard Broun in his *Memorabilia Curliana*, wrote of curlers as "the merry handlers of the *quoit*," and he once printed a letter written by Principal Baird of Edinburgh University to the famous Duddingston Club in 1822 in which the Principal stated that he wished to present the club with five specimens of the earliest *kuting* or *coiting*-stones. One of these was from Stirling while the other four were from the Loch of Linlithgow. These stones are from 3 to 4 inches in thickness, of rather an oblong shape, and thin towards the point extremity. At the opposite and thicker extremity there is on the bottom — which had been made smooth — a long, thin, hollow cut for admitting the forepart of the fingers, and in the upper side of the stone there is a hole for the end of the thumb. There were no dates on these stones, but a second discovery at about the same time affords ground for belief that the stones were very early specimens of the *kuting* type.

Turning now to a list of other stones we are told that about the year 1830 when the foundations of an old house at Strathallan were dug out a curling stone of a very different type and texture from the ones generally in use in that district was discovered. It was oblong in shape and had been neatly finished with a hammer. The initials "J. M." and the date, 1611, were quite legible. This discovery afforded the first proofs of the great antiquity of curling. Concerning this stone and its date our previously mentioned authority, Sir Richard Broun, put the significant query: "If a curling stone of an oblong form and neatly finished with a hammer gives the date, 1611, then what date will the *kuting* stone give?"

For a long time it was supposed that the oldest stone was one thus recorded in the *Annual* of 1841:

> This last summer a curling stone was found in an old curling pond near Dunblane bearing the date 1551. It is 10 inches broad by 11 inches long and 5 inches thick and seems to have been taken from the bed of the river and not to have been dressed. There are two holes for the handle as in the close-handled stones still preferred in the district.

This Dunblane stone, although an ancient one, was not of the primitive type, seeing that it had a handle, and therefore would seem to leave the query of Broun higher in the air than ever. But about seventy-five years ago a *kuting* stone of a date 100 years earlier than the Strathallan stone came to light and the Dunblane contender was in consequence forced to retire from the field. This new discovery, along with another of a like antique appearance, is now on view in the Macfarlane Museum in Stirling, and is still regarded, as far as we know, as the oldest curling stone in the world. Its shape (Fig. 2) is nearly oblong, the sides being straight and the top and bottom rounded. It is 9 inches long, 7½ inches wide and 4⅝ inches thick and weighs 26 pounds. The hole for the thumb (on the side not showing in the figure) is 1½ inches wide at the mouth, while the place for the fingers is 3½ inches. On the side not showing, a small space has been polished to receive the inscription in Roman capitals, "A GIFT", while on the sole is the following: "St.Js B. Stirling, 1511. It can only be surmised that "St.Js" stands for St.James, a one-time popular saint in Stirling, and "B" may stand either for "Bridge" or for "Brotherhood", there having been a St. James Hospital at the Bridge of Stirling, prior to the Reformation. The stone is made of blue whinstone, and having been a

Fig. 2

gift, was probably a fine specimen of the curling stone of
the time.

The second Stirling stone (Fig. 3), also of blue whin-
stone, was described by Captain Macnair in *The Channel
Stane* as appearing to be older and even more primitive, and
may have been originally a water-worn boulder taken from

Fig. 3

the bed of some stream. Its shape is
triangular, the sides and angles being rounded. It is 8¼ inches in
length, about the same in width,
depth 4 inches, circumference 22
inches, and weight 15¾ pounds. The
thumb-hole and finger-catch are
roughly cut. A search through the
records of the Museum (Macfarlane)
has failed to elicit any information
regarding the history of these stones.

Both Linlithgow and Lochleven were ancient homes of
curling, and the fact that curling in its early days was played
on the famous Lochleven Loch is confirmed by positive evidence. The very stone (Fig. 4) was taken from Lochleven

Fig. 4

more than a century ago. Its
shape has been compared,
humorously, to a small but
thick Belfast ham. As can
be seen, it never had a
handle, but has on its under
side, or sole, an oblong hollow for the player's fingers,
and on the upper side is a
corresponding hole for the
thumb. In the figure it is shown as standing somewhat on
end.

Figure 5 shows another *kuting* stone that was found in 1826 at Roslin, whose chief glory lies in its chapel, so finely described in Scott's *Lay of the Last Minstrel*.

Fig. 5

Figure 6 is also a genuine type of the early *kutings*, but as it once belonged to a well known Covenanter named Guthrie, it must have been in use after 1644 when he was ordained as minister

Fig. 6

of Fenwick. The upper or thumb hole, and the two lower hollows for the spreading fingers (all showing in the figure) give us a clear idea of how those *kuting* stones were sent gliding along the ice.

Considering all that those auld, auld stanes tell us in the way of shapes, holds and dates, the *kuting* period may safely be set down as extending from the beginning of the sixteenth century to the middle of the seventeenth. The handled type of stone, too, was used in that period.

The reason the *kuting* stone with its thumb and finger holds was finally compelled, after 150 years of use, to give way to the channel-stone is easily understood. In fact it is remarkable that this early type lasted as long as it did, there being so much against it. For instance, it was a physical impossibility to deliver a *kuting* stone properly with the player's fingers gripping the under side. With such a handicap there was no other way to deliver the stone than by swinging it from behind and then giving it a short throw forward, ending in a final thrust. It didn't matter at how fine an angle the player might have "floored" his stone, this "chance" delivery would always have been far behind the perfectly balanced Swing-Slide Delivery practised to-day. Nor was this its only disadvantage. The *kuting* stone was largely unplayable when over 25 pounds in weight, unless the player had the strongest of hands.

The handle must have been thought of by many in those older days; but people (especially rural) are as a rule conservative—slow to change, and so in curling. But once the handle came into use the stone had to be thicker in order to furnish depth for the iron upright of the handle to be inserted and made fast deep down in the upper side. An increase in weight, too, would come by degrees, as the advantages of weight became more and more evident from experience. And where would those old-time curlers have gone, instinctively, to seek for smooth and suitably shaped stones, but to the channels of rivers and brooks where nature had been grinding them smooth for thousands of years? Thus, it unquestionably must have come about that our curling forefathers became possessed of the channel-stone whose handle made possible a natural delivery and whose delivery, in turn, made possible the elbow-out and elbow-in, which in their turn completed the task of establishing curling as one of the outstanding sports in the world.

As the two accompanying figures make clear, the first of the channel-stones were about the same size as the *kutings*. At an exhibition held in Glasgow in 1888 the Marquis of Breadalbane placed on view an ancient pair of stones which had been taken out of Newton Loch near Tyndrum, around 1860, while the loch was being drained preparatory to making it safer for curling. Though the weights of the

Fig. 7

Breadalbane pair were about the
same as some better known *kutings*, the single holes (Figures 7
and 8) were evidently made for
handles, and this would place them
(considering their small size) as

Fig. 8

belonging among the first channel-stones. Comparing the
earlier type of those iron-handled stones with the polished
articles used today, we cannot fail to realize how great the
advance has been. A writer thus describes the earlier types.

> They were of a wretched description enough; many of them
> being sea-stones of all sizes, shapes, and weights. Some were
> three-cornered like those equilateral cocked hats which our
> divines wore in a century that is past. Others like ducks,
> others flat as a frying pan. Their handles were equally clumsy
> and unelegant, being malconstructed resemblances of that
> hook-necked bird, the goose.

Ungainly as those types are in appearance, hunters
of curling relics covet them, each hoping to become the
proud owner of the very ugliest; and this desire, of
course, goes back to the *kutings.* Many were giants as to
size and only giants could ever
have handled them. A stone was
found embedded many years ago
when along with others it was
dug up on the draining of Ardoch
Pond on the estate of Mr. Drum-
mond Moray. It is dated 1700 and
bears letters, "M.W.H." In the interesting records of the Muthill
Club which go back to 1739 the

Fig. 9

first name there entered is "The Rev. Mr. William Hally, Minister, Muthill". Consequently this stone has always been regarded as having belonged to that divine in view of the fact
that the carved initials suggest the name, and that he was the
first minister of Muthill after the abolition of the Episcopacy

in 1690. This stone has a three-legged handle and is today the property of the Royal Caledonian Club.

Fig. 10                    Fig. 11

Fig. 12

Fig. 13                    Fig. 14

Figures 10, 11, 12, 13, 14 show what is perhaps the most interesting and widely-known group of stones to be found in all Scotland. They passed by sale or presentation from the Blairgowrie Club to the Delvine Club. Figure 10, the "Soo", portrays a stone which weighs 79 pounds and measures 16½ by 11 inches. "The Baron" (Fig. 11) weighs 88 pounds and measures 14½ by 14 inches. Figure 12, appropriately named "The Egg", pictures a stone weighing 115 pounds and measuring 17 by 12 inches. "The Fluke" (Fig. 13) weighs 52 pounds and measures 12½ by 11 inches. And "Robbie Dow" (Fig. 14), called after the minister's son, weighs only 34 pounds, a mere infant, and measures 9 by 9 inches.

Authorities are inclined to think that they were taken in a natural state from the famous Ericht Channel. In the following Centenary Ode by a Mr. Bridie, poet of the Blairgowrie Club, four of these stones are mentioned:

Fig. 15

> *In early years the implements were coarse,*
> *Rude, heavy boulders did the duty then;*
> *And each one had its title as "The Horse":*
> *One was "The Cockit Hat" and one "The Hen"*
> *"The Kirk", "The Saddle", "President" and "Soo"*
> *"The Bannock", "Baron", "Fluke" and "Robbie Dow".*

Figure 15 shows a hand-chipped, somewhat conically shaped stone, "The Black Meg". Meg weighs 66 pounds. Note the shape of this stone as foreshadowing the coming of the all-round circular stone destined to drive the boulders off the ice.

Figure 16 shows one of the several stones found in 1881 at Lochlane near Crieff on Lord Abercrombie's estate of Ferntower. This stone is also in the possession of the Royal Caledonian Club and also shows an approach in shape to the modern circular stone.

Fig. 16

Figure 17 with the letter "W" cut into its upper surface, is from Birkhill Pond near Stirling. The hole for the handle is there but not the handle itself. Two other handle-equipped stones bearing the respective titles of "The Provost" and "The Bailie" and weighing about 60

Fig. 17

pounds each, are on view at Dunblane; while at Jedburgh are two others bearing the less impressive titles of "The Girdle" and "The Grey Hen".

In addition to possessing the "Guthrie" stone, already mentioned, the Muthill Club also possesses a square-block of a stone (Fig. 18) called "The Bible". This stone may have

been thus reverently named from its slightly bookish appearance possibly reminding a one-time Presbyterian owner of the big ha' Bible seen by him on each Sabbath morn, high placed on the pulpit cushion. Or perhaps its name may have been due to a reverent super-

Fig. 18

stition that a curling stone so named could never be "*lickit*".

It is not difficult to understand how "The Goose" received its name (Fig. 19). Geese and ducks being crooked-necked birds, curling stones with similar crooked handles

became endowed with their names.

Figure 20, "T h e Grey Mare", is a good example of the "closed-handle" s t o n e. The three empty holes on the top were probably due to previous failures in setting the handle to give the true balance.

Fig. 19

Fig. 21 is the last of the mighty specimens of giant stones. This stone was called "The Jubilee Stone", having been presented as a gift from John Wilson, Cockburnspath, to the Royal Caledonian Curling

Fig. 20

Club, on the occasion of its
Jubilee Celebration, July 25th,
1888. It weighs 117 pounds
and was originally the property of one, John Hood, a keen
curler who had died only a
few months before that Jubilee

Fig. 21

meeting. Mr. Hood used to relate, said Dr. Kerr, that he had
seen his father play this huge stone and that he himself had
played it occasionally before dressed stones were introduced.
Mr. Wilson, when presenting the great stone, stated that
when such toys were used by his own and John Hood's forebears, "the gude wife of the farmer used herself to carry to
the pond a bicker of brose made with the 'broo' of beef and
greens being prepared for dinner", where, after play was
over, all adjoined to discuss the beef and greens and to fight
their battles again over a few tumblers of toddy.

Though in a far lesser degree the men at that long past
curling dinner were the same in spirit as was that toddy-
inspired Warrior King, The Great Alexander, who as glorious
old John Dryden wrote:

*Fought all his battles o'er again
And thrice he routed all his foes and thrice he slew the slain.*

Sir Richard Broun gives 1750 as the approximate time
when the first regularly formed circular stone stood upon
Scottish ice. Dr. Cairnie, touching on the same subject, says
that, about 1770, stones were still variously shaped, few of
them so perfectly rounded as to be admissible on the rinks
of 1883 and with some still triangular in form. One of these
called "The Cockit Hat", was so truly formidable that unless
hit full it would not move from the spot but rotated in great
perfection. Still another authority on curling tells of an
occasion when a player borrowed a shoemaker's lapstone

Fig. 22

Fig. 23

which gave him such an advantage that the others declined to play with him.

One of the earliest of the better formed circular type (Fig. 22) was a stone which closely resembled the mason's mallet as known in 1844. This picture is taken from an old woodcut published in 1810.

Sir Richard Broun described in his book a conically-shaped stone (Fig. 23), broad at the bottom and gradually tapering upwards. It first came into use at Dunblane and was said to have been a smooth runner and of sufficient height that the player need not stoop low down to reach the handle. This handle was closed at both ends so that it could be safely swung from the fingers.

Of the next group, the first has the form of a semi-

Fig. 24        Fig. 25        

Fig. 26

inflated balloon under a pressing weight. Considerable pains were taken in the adornment (Fig. 25), while the last of the group (Fig. 26), depicts a stone which (judging from those depicted in Sir George Harvey's famous painting, "The Curlers") goes well back into the eighteenth century.

"The Cheese" is a well-known stone which not only stands as a representative of a class but has a little history of its own. It was one of a rink of stones made over a century and a half ago from a large block of whinstone cut out of Thornton Hall quarry, Lanarkshire. It weighs 70 pounds (Fig. 27). The last match in which it figured was 107 years ago, when it was used as a first stone. As its master was the only one on the ice who, with certainty, could send the stone to the tee, he practically won the match with it. After matches it was often used as a test of strength, and at other times it functioned in the weighing of oatmeal and cheese! Finally, it was one of

Fig. 27

the stones on the table at the Jubilee Celebration banquet at the R.C.C.C. in 1888.

A few of the earlier circular stones are noted either for their special markings or on account of their one-time titled owners. Two of such, still on view at Penicuick House, were played by their owner, Sir James Clerk in the latter half of the eighteenth century. As shown, Fig. 28 bore the imprint of a star and was known as "The Star", while Fig. 29, carrying the family horn was known as "The Horn".

Fig. 28

Fig. 29

Given over to the keeping of the Ardgowan Club in 1880, and still on view there, is the stone once owned and played by "The King o' a' The Core", Tam Samson, The Man o' Kilmarnoch, immortalized by Robbie Burns. The stone is naturally one of great interest not only as a memorial but also as a marked example of the earlier part of the third period. It is now almost solely used in the initiation of new members and is decked by a silver plate fixed on its upper side and bearing the inscription, "TAM SAMSON'S STANE, PRESENTED BY PETER MORRISON TO THE ARDGOWAN CURLING CLUB, 1857".

Its weight is 54½ pounds; circumference 35¾ inches; and height 6⅛ inches. The handle is made of iron with a distance clear of the stone measuring 1 inch. (See Fig. 30).

The next illustration (Fig. 31) is taken from a steel engraving found in an edition

Fig. 30

of Scott's *Guy Mannering*. The outside stones, one with a closed handle and the other with an open handle, bear each a marked resemblance to like handled stones in the Harvey painting; while the middle stone somewhat resembles "Black Meg" (Fig. 15), a resemblance that would place it as belonging to an even earlier date than that of its two com-

Fig. 31                                        Fig. 32

panions. The stones in Fig. 32 have an individuality of their own. From the locality wherein they were found, it is more than likely that they belonged to one or other of the clubs which in the long ago operated just outside the old Town of Edinburgh and are probably as odd specimens of the circular stone as can be found. The stone with the ring handle, by which it was swung to the ice, is in a class by itself. The two remaining are of the earlier circular type, but have the old channel-stone handles which would seem to class them as belonging to that part of the transition period before the circular stones had become fully dominant on the curling ponds and lochs of Scotland.

Fig. 33, a modern curling stone, is composed of the famous Scotch granite.

Fig. 33

## The Various Foot Accoutrements Once Widely
### Used by the Scottish Curler

The Scottish curler, especially in times before rubber or felt-soled boots came into existence, had to find other means of providing himself with a firm footing or brace when delivering or sweeping a stone. The oldest foot accoutrement was known as the *crampit,* also called *crampbit, crampet, cramp* or *tramp.* As shown (Fig. 34), it is a thin iron or steel plate with teeth across the under surface and was bound to the foot with straps like an old-time skate.

Fig. 34—Crampits

The second invention with its variation, (Fig. 35) is called the *Currie Crampit* and is rather ingenious. The clamps can be tightened by turning a screw-bolt connecting the two ends.

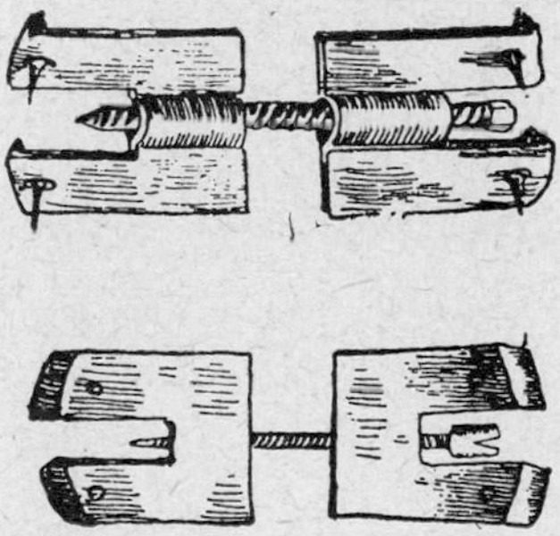

Fig. 35—Currie Crampits

Dr. Cairnie, the first president of the Royal Caledonian Club, condemned the use of cram-

Fig. 36

pits as "almost barbarous," as they certainly must have been
to the ice, and by his invention of the foot-iron (Fig. 36) with
its file-like surface provided a contrivance that gradually
displaced them.

The Cairnie foot-iron was credited not only with the dis-
placement of the crampits but also of other kinds of foot-gear
which in number of patterns would seem to have been turned
out by a corresponding number of clubs. These went by the
general name of *trickers* and need only to be pictured (Figures 37 to 44 inclusive) to be clearly understood. All were
made to serve as braces for the entire foot. Figure 41, probably the work of a curling blacksmith, seems to have been
made by adding to and sharpening the caulks of an old horse-

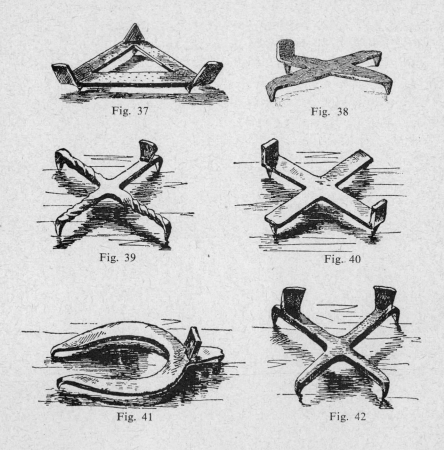

Fig. 37

Fig. 38

Fig. 39

Fig. 40

Fig. 41

Fig. 42

Fig. 43                                          Fig. 44

shoe. All these devices were necessary. Either a foot-board (Fig. 46) or some kind of a tricker were once indis-pensable to the curlers of Scotland seeing that "hacks" were—and in some districts still are—largely taboo, due to the fact that the prevailing thinness of the ice on many ponds and lochs renders deep cuttings therein inadvisable. For should hacks be cut too deep, water oozes up and plays the *"verra deil wi' the game"*.

Scientific curl-ing as we know it today would have been impossible with the stones used during the second period. In the diagram here shown, devised by Dr. Kerr, please note that on the left the stones are all ir-regular in shape —the channel-stone type. Stone B lies just outside the lower right-hand quarter of

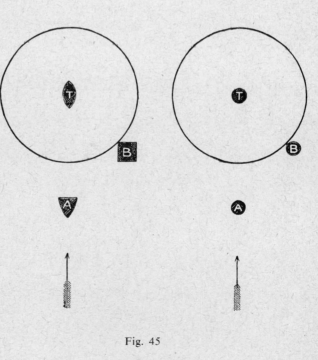

Fig. 45

Circle No. 1: and an oval-shaped stone on the tee is guarded by an angular stone A. These are both enemy stones and the player with another malformed stone is about to attempt to remove the shot on the tee and lie shot himself. He has three ways: he can attempt to draw around A with sufficient speed to remove the shot; or he can try to wick and curl in off B—a stone belonging to his own side; or he can try with an outwick to send B in on the tee stone. But to succeed with a draw what chance, outside of a mere fluke, would he have with his malformed stone, of so accurately estimating his strength, even though he played the broom to a hair, as to reach T with the speed required? Not one chance in fifty. Or suppose he should try to wick and curl in off B? In this attempt, granting his stone to be of the 50-odd pounds variety, he could go all out in the way of "commin' a thunnerin" yet in all likelihood it would only be a case of angle hitting angle with both stones flying every which way. And had he tried outwicking, the result would have been the same or worse.

Many of those old channel-stone players used to shift their place for delivery far enough over to the right or left to give them a clear path to otherwise well guarded shots. We are told that this side-stepping was considered bad form. Yet it was done. In those swash-buckling times, the "king o' a' the core" was the crack marksman, the curler with blood in his eye, who liked nothing better than to receive an order such as might be given to some fictitious Sandy

Fig. 46

MacDuff (Fig. 46) "to come a thunnerin and clear the hoose". Such a Sandy could doubtless have qualified as the equal of the immortal Tam Samson in the way of roarin' up the rink, but he would probably have fallen far below the level of the then unborn Tam, when essaying with the stone he had "to guard or draw or wick a bore".

The outcome of the same problem with the stones used in Circle No. 2 can safely be left to the judgment of a curling reader who will know as well as the writer, that to remove shot T would, to a skilful hand, only be an incident in the day's work.

The greater efficiency of the modern stone when pitted against the old channel-stone may be appreciated by allowing the two—the auld and the noo—to stand face to face solely for the purpose of contrast. (Fig. 47.)

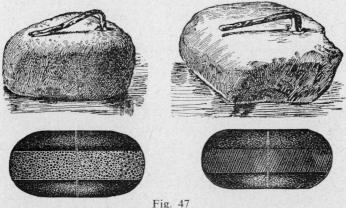

Fig. 47

What a marvellous change for the better has been brought to pass down through the years! Of the curling stone of the twentieth century it can be truly said, that no other game given to man has had a more adaptable instrument. The stone which we now use, when delivered from the curler's hand, becomes at once a living and a sentient thing into which the spirit and the purpose of the player have passed.

# CHAPTER VI

## HOW CURLING STONES
## ARE FASHIONED

*Auld channel-stanes were found along the shore*
*O' lochs and rivers, streams and wanton brooks;*
*Now men wi' mighty drills the centres bore*
*O' granite blocks and then quick pass them o'er*
*To ither brawny chiels who in a trice*
*Gie each its balance, shape and polished locks*
*Before it ever comes upon the ice.*

ROBERT BURNS, IN HIS DAY, PUT AILSA CRAIG DOWN AS STONE
deaf in his lines on the disconsolate wooer, Duncan Grey and
Duncan's unresponsive Meg:

*Duncan fleech'd and Duncan pray'd,*
*Ha, Ha, the wooing o't;*
*Meg was deaf as Ailsa Craig,*
*Ha, Ha, the wooing o't.*

And the imaginative John Keats, sitting in front of the
little inn at Girvan on a certain sunny afternoon in the early
part of the last century, looked across the Firth of Clyde at
the lonely mountain of Ailsa Craig, and as a consequence
became sufficiently moved to write the following sonnet:

*Hearken thou craggy ocean pyramid!*
*Give answer from thy voice—the sea-fowl's screams!*
*When were thy shoulders mantled in huge streams?*
*When from the sun was thy proud forehead hid?*
*How long is't since the mighty power bid*
*Thee heave in airy sleep from fathom dreams?*

84

*Sleep in the lap of thunder or sun beams,*
*Or when grey clouds are thy cold coverlid?*
*Thou answer'st not, for thou art dead asleep.*
  *Thy life is but two dead eternities—*
*The last in air, the former in the deep;*
*First with the whales, last in the eagle skies—*
*Drown'd wast thou till an earthquake made thee steep,*
*Another cannot wake thy giant size.*

Ailsa Craig is a veritable mountain of granite. Charles Darwin, in *The Voyage of the Beagle,* tells of having examined, in 1834, the granite masses of Chili's "Très Montes" and then in conclusion comments on the mystery of the rock itself:

> Granite has given rise, perhaps, to more discussion concerning its origin than any other formation. We generally see it constituting the fundamental rock, and, however formed, we know it is the deepest layer in the crust of this globe to which man has penetrated.

Webster's *Dictionary* includes the following geological data:

> In geology, an aggregate rock composed of the minerals, quartz, feldspar, and mica, or at least two of these minerals confusedly crystallized together. The texture is more or less finely granular. The grains vary in size from that of a pinhead to a mass of two or three feet; but usually the largest size is that of a nut. The colour of granite is greatly diversified by the different colours and proportions of the component parts, and in general these stones are VERY HARD. The most common colours are grey, greyish-white, and flesh-red.

The earliest report, as far back as 1549, concerning Ailsa Craig, is that its sole inhabitants were solan geese. It was later, well into the time of Keats, that a meagre shipping of granite for curling stones began to be carried on.

Possibly impressed by the facts recorded above, young curlers as well as old may be moved to look with a greater respect upon their individual pairs of curling stones. A series of processes must be carried out before the rough blocks from the cliff granite of Ailsa Craig are converted into curling stones. A traveller by sea when a few miles out from the mouth of the Clyde may hear, away to the left, the sound of an explosion; this would probably be due to blasting operations from the cliff face of Ailsa Craig, destined to bring the resulting fragments of granite down upon the beach. And were our assumed traveller by sea able and sufficiently curious to visit that island on the following day, he might come upon a scene showing masses of the recently blasted granite, after having been divided into blocks marked in numbers, being loaded for shipment.

The entire island would seem to be nothing but granite down to the sea level. The dimensions of Ailsa Craig may give us some conception of how much of this curling material is ultimately obtainable: its height is over 1,100 feet; its length, 3,900 feet; its width nearly 2,500 feet; while its circumference, enclosing a surface of 220 acres, is 2¼ miles. At an annual output of 1,000 pairs of blocks, rating twelve to a ton, the question is frequently raised as to the length of time needed to blast the entire island down to the sea thus rashly exposing (as some would jocularly have us believe) the throat of a suppressed volcano, liable—when freed from the island's weight—to erupt and bury all Scotland.

It is a comfort to know, however, that curling enthusiasts who recently visited Scotland, report that today, some of the stone used in the manufacture of curling stones, although essentially the same as that from Ailsa, is obtained from other parts of the country.

Ailsa Craig is rented by the granite shippers from the Marquis of Ailsa. On a special visit to the island some years ago, Dr. Kerr was able to witness the initial processes toward the production of curling stones at first hand. Now although times have changed, we are able to report that much the same processes are in use today. Dr. Kerr reported that the boss workman, called the blocker-general, is the man through whose hands the majority of the granite blocks pass; that a

particular knowledge as to what blocks are naturally suitable
for matched pairs is largely an acquired knowledge; that simi-
larities in boulders must be recognized, not always an easy
task; and that, when recognized, such boulders are roughly
reduced to sizes required and then each is chipped to a satisfactory squareness. The two blocks thus treated are given the
same number in plainly marked figures. The final matching
of pairs, however, as far as successful pairing is possible,
is left to the several manufacturers to whom the blocks, properly marked, are shipped. Also, as curlers in general now
know, there are three kinds of Ailsas—the Blue Hone, the
Red Hone, and the Common Hone. The last named, however, is not considered as an inferior stone, since the word
"common" simply means that compared to the other two
it is easier to get at. The Red Hone has, with every passing
year, become harder to procure. It was found high up on
the face of the cliff, and to extract it the workmen have had
to descend from the summit on a rope line and insert a time
blast. The difficulty in getting it out accounts for its high
price; but actually the authorities give Blue Hone the
preference both over the Red and the so-called Common
Ailsas.

All three, however, are obliged to go through the same
rough handling. When properly divided the roughly squared
blocks are taken by boat to Girvan whence they are dis-
patched to the manufacturies. There the blocks are first
chiselled or cheesed (i.e. shaped somewhat like a cheese);
and that done, the stones are bored, and when properly balanced are passed, one by one, into the hands of a workman.
With a toothed hammer he gives each a rough all-round
finish before it is rolled off with a mould. (This process is
done by machine today.)

The stone, no longer a crude block, is then sent to the
grinding machine. This machine consists of two parts. The
stone, immovably clamped within a cup-like container at the

end of the vertical shaft, is whirled around at great speed by means of a large upper belt, which, assisted by two smaller belts, one on each side of a vertical wheel intercogging with a horizontally placed mate, give altogether (the three belts working in unison) the concentrated power needed to enable the horizontal cogwheel to turn a vertical shaft which turns the cup-shaped container. This holds the curling stone hard down on the great steam-powered grinder, inexorably turning it through an angle of about ninety degrees.

By this simple but thoroughly effective process the stone is quickly made to take the shape required and to become at the same time considerably smoothed.

The next process is the grinding out of the small circular hollow in the centre of the running sole. This is accomplished by placing the stone directly over a raised edge on the surface of the grinder. In that first grinding process the stone, by means of a lever made to raise the cup-shaped container, can at any time be taken out and another inserted with the machine still kept running at the usual speed. But in this second process both parts of the machine are slowed down so as to prevent any possible injury to the keen running edge which surrounds the concave area; since that would make the stone useless as far as curling is concerned.

When this running edge is completed, the stone is fixed within a second cup-shaped container and is there whirled around at tremendous speed by a concealed power belt working underneath. The stone here goes through three processes of honing. The materials used are, first the rough freestone; then the Crakesland stone (carborundum is usually substituted today); and for the third, the Water of Ayr hone. Each is successively applied by hand to both the upper and the lower sides. When all this has been done the upper side can be looked upon as finished. But to the lower area a polishing putty is applied by using a piece of flannel held firmly on a now heated stone, a heating which possibly allows it to absorb the polish into its very grain. Not yet, however, can the stone be considered as completely finished, seeing that there still remains a belt of rough surface encircling the larger circumference, a surface that must be ornately levelled. This is a task which demands a special tool. With a diamond cutter two lines are marked around the entire circumference, one line marking the lower edge of this rough belt and the other marking the upper edge. This encircling space between the marked lines is then chiselled into a neat band which in many a hard fought game to come will receive the knockout and the chap-in-lie shots and "be nane a bit the waur for a' that". Is the stone now completed? Not quite. It has still to be equipped with an iron bolt, square-headed on the lower end so as to fit tight within a like squared cavity cut out in the exact centre of the running sole. The upper end of this bolt, whose length extends through the bored centre of the stone and a little beyond, is threaded to fit similar threading within a shallow perforation with a prominent outer edge, all made in the exact under-centre of a circular, polished-steel plate to which an arched handle ending in THE GRIP, is attached. (The modern grips or handles are made of plastic. At one time they were bone or ivory and often richly mounted with silver.) This inner-threaded perforation beneath the steel plate, when fitted on top of the protruding bolt end and kept turning, will corkscrew its downward way round and round the similarly threaded bolt end until the underside of the steel plate has been screwed flat down against the smooth, flat surface of the stone's upper side. When like has thus become inter-threaded with like to the last possible turning of the plate, then will a completely finished and fully equipped CURLING STONE stand ready for THE ICE.

# CHAPTER VII

## CURLING AS CELEBRATED
## BY THE BARDS

*Poetry is of all human learnings the most ancient, and of the most fatherly antiquity, as from whence other learnings have taken their beginnings, since it is so universal that no learned nation doth despise it, nor barbarous nation is without it.*

SIR PHILIP SIDNEY

THE POEMS AND SINGLE VERSES on curling and curlers (except for a few pieces of my own) are taken, in the main, from early books on curling, and many of them appeared in Dr. Kerr's *History of Curling*.

As far as can be ascertained, the first rhymes about curling are to be found in an old poetical lament entitled *The Muses Threnodie*, completed in 1620 and published in Edinburgh eighteen years later. The author was Henry Adamson, and James Gall whose death was the subject of the lament, was a one-time merchant of Perth. In this Scottish elegy a George Ruthven, Physician & Surgeon, and close friend of both Adamson and Gall, is purportedly the chief mourner. Ruthven in his leisure hours enjoyed, along with other sports, the game of curling. So in this old Threnodie the poet, referring to Ruthven's professional and sporting accessories, thus writes:

*His hats, his hoods, his bels, his bones,*
*His allay bowles and curling stones,*
*The sacred games to celebrat,*
*Which to the gods are consecrat.*

And farther on we read:

*And for your part the trible to you take,*
*And when you cry make all your crags to crake,*
*And shiver when you sing alace for Gall!*
*Ah if our mourning might thee now recall!*
*And yee my Loadstones of Lidnochian Lakes,*
*Collected from the loughs where watrie snakes*
*Do much abound, take unto you a part,*
*And mourn for Gall who lov'd you with his heart.*

Still again:

*How can I choose but mourn? when I think on*
*Our games Olympike-like, in times agone.*

Those loadstones of Lidnochian Lakes were curling stones of the channel type taken from Lake Lidnoch four miles from Perth; and the George Ruthven of the poem is now regarded as the earliest curler of whom a genuine record exists. He was ninety-two years of age when the poem was published and was therefore already an old man when Adamson wrote of him and his loadstones of Lidnochian lakes mourning over the death of Gall in 1620. George Ruthven is said to have taught his fellow citizens both by precept and example that curling could make men cheerful workers and "jolly good fellows."

In the curling records of the seventeenth century the name Ruthven was followed by the names of two divines. For as an old Scotch proverb has it—"Frae Maidenkirk to John o' Groats nae curlers like the clergy".

During the eighteenth century curling retained its place in literature. Allan Ramsay was a genuine curling poet who in an epistle to Robert Yarde of Devonshire thus rhymed:

*Frae northern mountains clad with snaw,*
*Where whistling winds incessant blaw,*

*In time now when the curling stane*
*Slides murmuring o'er the icy plain.*

And in another poem on *Health* he makes a second reference to curling:

*From ice with pleasure he can brush the snow*
*And run rejoicing with his curling throw.*

Nothing in the way of a literary reference belonging to the eighteenth century will ever be regarded as superior to these inimitable verses on curling by Robbie Burns, Scotland's bard of bards, in that widely known *Elegy on Tam Samson* (1786), wherein he presents to the world his friend, Samson, as having long been the premier skip on the ponds of auld Kilmarnock:

*When winter muffles up his cloak,*
*And binds the mire like a rock;*
*When to the loughs the curlers flock*
*Wi' gleesome speed,*
*Wha will they station at the cock?*
*Tam Samson's dead!*

*He was the king o' a' the core*
*To guard, or draw, or wick a bore,*
*Or up the rink like Jehu roar*
*In time o' need;*
*But now he lags on Death's "hog score"*
*Tam Samson's dead!*

The very curling stone used by the sport-loving old Tam in the above mentioned "guarding", "drawing" and "wicking" is pictured in Figure 30, Page 78.

Yet when the above lines were written poor Tam was "no deid". In fact, as a well-to-do seedsman in Kilmarnock he is known to have out-lived that first publication of the *Elegy* by nine years; and though fully appreciating the encomiums penned by his friend, Burns, as to his acknowledged standing in the social and sporting life of the community, Old Tam so keenly resented the fifteen-times repeated assurance that he, Tam, was beyond all question *deid*, that on the next occasion of his meeting the poet, he is reported, after proffering his thanks for the praises given him, to have concluded with these pathetic words: "But Rabbie, mon, I'm no deid yet!"

Greatly moved by the evident concern of his old friend and crony, and as a way of rectifying a wrong unwittingly done, Burns immediately sat down and wrote the following, now world famous:

### PER CONTRA

*Go, Fame, and canter like a filly,*
*Through a' the streets an' neuks o'Killy;*
*Tell every social honest billie*
*To cease his grievin'*
*For yet unskaith'd by Death's gleg gullie,*
*Tam Samson's leevin'!*

A pathetic little poem entitled *My Bonny Broomy Kowe* appeared in the *Annual* of the Grand Caledonian Curling Club in the middle of the nineteenth century and was written by W. A. Peterkin. The Scottish curlers consider the "kowe" to have a truly national significance as a curling essential but look upon the ordinary house brooms as things fit only for the kitchen.

### MY BONNY BROOMY KOWE

#### Tune: The Nameless Lassie

*In summers past I've seen thee bloom*
*On mossy banks and knowe;*
*I've revelled mid thy sweet perfume,*
*My bonny broomy kowe.*
*I've garlanded thy yellow flowers,*
*I've lain beneath thy bough;*
*I' ll ne'er forget thy youthful prime,*
*My bonny broomy kowe.*

*You've been my friend at ilka spiel,*
*You've polished up the howe,*
*You've mony a stane brocht owre the hog,*

*My bonny broomy kowe.*
*As mem'ry noo recalls the past,*
    *My heart is set alowe,*
*Wi' moistened e'en I gaze on thee,*
    *My bonny broomy kowe.*

*Time tells on a'; your pith has gane,*
    *And wrinkled is my brow;*
*We're nae sae fresh as we hae been,*
    *My bonny broomy kowe.*
*You're wizzen'd sair, and maist as thin*
    *As hairs upon my pow,*
*I doubt our days are nearly dune,*
    *My bonny broomy kowe.*

*When death comes o'er me, let my grave*
    *Be sacred frae the plough;*
*For cypress plant a golden broom,*
    *That yet may be a kowe.*
*Nor rest nor peace shall e'er be yours—*
    *A' curlers hear my vow—*
*Unless there grows abune my head*
    *A bonny broomy kowe.*

The following four lines are such as one can feel were written straight from the heart:

*True feelings waken in our hearts*
*And thrill frae heart to han';*
*O peerless game that feeds the flame*
*O' fellowship in man!*

REV. T. RAIN

Mr. James Millar, a one-time leading member of the famous Duddingston Club, expressed in the verses given below his great love of curling:

*Such are my joys, yet one dearer unsung*
*The bold Caledonian claims for his own;*
*'Tis when winter her white robe o'er Arthur has flung,*
*And the loch at its base under icy chains thrown.*

*Then eager we haste, with the slow-rising sun,*
*To enter the lists on the slippery vale;*
*Where defiance to combat, or prize to be won,*
*Prolongs the fond strife until darkness assail.*

*How ardent the conflict when curlers engage!*
*The keen piercing north wind unheeded may blow;*
*Let the cit or the coxcomb fly trembling his rage;*
*No feeling have those but to vanquish the foe.*

*Nor inglorious the wreath that the victors entwine;*
*'Tis the meed of sage counsel which brilliant deeds crown;*
*Just eye, steady nerves, active strength must combine*
*With devotion to toil and a love of renown.*

*Now the well-polished whin-stone wins calmly its way*
*With nicest momentum in the ring to repose;*
*Now strikes like a bolt, as resistless its sway,*
*Yet the guidance so sure, it strikes only its foes.*

*But who can describe the still varying game?*
*New efforts, new schemes, every movement demands,*
*Tho' each change but augments the enthusiast's flame,*
*And each crisis loud praise or censure commands.*

*And oft it will chance, as the doubtful war burns,*
*That victory rests on one high-fated blow;*
*Hope and fear fill the combatants' bosoms by turns;*
*These pray it may hit; those that erring it go.*

*All eyes bend on him who decides the great stake;*
*Dread pause! the stone's sped. Hark! "He has it", they cry.*
*"He has it" resounds throughout Duddingston Lake,*
*And the rocks of proud Arthur, "He has it", reply.*

*Thus passes the day; ah! too brief. Yet belong*
*Other charms to the eve; then the feast and the bowl,*
*Feats recounted or threatened, the laugh and the song,*
*Till social delights pervade every soul.*

Among the early nineteenth century verses is a song composed by Sir Alexander Boswell, which rendered in "braid" Scotch, was said to have been received with unreserved applause by the Duddingston Society:

*Let feckless chiels like crucket weans,*
*Gae blaw their thums wi' pechs and granes,*
*Or thaw their fushionless shank banes,*
*    And hurkle at an ingle.*

*But lads o' smeddum croose and bauld*
*Whase bluid can thole a nip o' cauld,*
*Your ice stanes in your gray plaids fauld*
*    And try on lochs a pingle.*

CHORUS:
> *When snaw lies white on ilka knowe,*
> *The ice stane and the guid broom kowe,*
> *Can warm us like a bleezin' lowe,*
> *Fair fa' the ice and curlin'!*

James Grahame, a well known early nineteenth century poet, in lauding the winter delights of Duddingston Loch in a poem entitled *January*, concluded with what is regarded as one of the finest descriptions of a bonspiel:

> *Now rival parishes and shrievedoms keep*
> *On upland lochs the long expected tryst*
> *To play their yearly bonspiel. Aged men,*
> *Smit with the eagerness of youth, are there,*
> *While love of conquest lights their beamless eyes,*
> *New-nerves their arms, and makes them young once more.*
>
> *The sides when ranged, the distance meted out,*
> *And duly traced the tees, some younger hand*
> *Begins with throbbing heart and far o'ershoots,*
> *Or sideward leaves, the mark; in vain he bends*
> *His waist, and winds his hand, as if it still*
> *Retained the power to guide the devious stone,*
> *Which, onward hurling, makes the circling groupe*
> *Quick start aside, to shun its reckless force.*
> *But more and still more skilful arms succeed,*
> *And near and nearer still around the tee,*
> *This side, now that, approaches; till at last*
> *Two, seeming equidistant, straws or twigs*
> *Decide as umpires 'tween contending coits.*
> *Keen, keener still, as life itself were staked,*
> *Kindles the friendly strife; one points the line*
> *To him who, poising, aims and aims again;*
> *Another runs and sweeps where nothing lies.*
> *Success alternately, from side to side,*
> *Changes; and quick the hours un-noted fly,*
> *Till light begins to fail, and deep below,*
> *The player, as he stoops to lift his coit,*
> *Sees, half incredulous, the rising moon.*
> *But now the final, the decisive spell,*
> *Begins; near and more near the sounding stones,*
> *Some winding in, some bearing straight along,*

*Crowd jostling all around the mark, while one,*
*Just slightly touching, victory depends*
*Upon the final aim; long swings the stone,*
*Then with full force, careering furious on,*
*Rattling, it strikes aside both friend and foe,*
*Maintains its course, and takes the victor's place.*

*The social meal succeeds, and social glass;*
*In words the fight renewed is fought again,*
*While festive mirth forgets the winged hours—*
*Some quit betimes the scene and find that home*
*Is still the place where genuine pleasure dwells.*

Next we are given some concluding lines of another nineteenth century poem, written by Captain Paterson, in which he praised the skill of a Bailie Hamilton:

*A better drawer ne'er clapped foot in natch;*
*He once, near Bothwell Brig, with dextrous cunning,*
*Drew through a ten-inch port for three times running;*
*The rink in length was forty yards and nine,*
*As measured by Tam Haddow with his line;*
*And when the stone they in the port did place,*
*On neither side was there an inch of space;*
*The ice in length was forty-two yards good*
*Down from the pass to where the bailie stood;*
*The plaudits loud from lookers-on and all,*
*Alarmed "The Douglas" in his castle hall.*

John Cairnie, president of the Royal Caledonian Curling Club, was not only an ardent curler but one who was kind to the poor and a favourite with all who knew him. The following elegy, written by his close friend, Captain Paterson, makes fitting reference to his fine qualities and to the wide sense of grief occasioned by his death:

*Why droops the banner half-mast high,*
*And curlers heave the bitter sigh?*
*Why throughout Largs the tearful eye,*
    *So blear'd and red?*
*Oh! listen to the poor man's cry!*
    *John Cairnie's dead!*

*While winter's breath as waters freeze,*
*Lays waste the fields and bares the trees,*
*Or well-rigged yachts in joyous breeze*
*For prizes ply,*
*Cairnie! Thy name by land or seas*
*Shall never die.*

As Dr. Kerr stated, "it seems to have been the custom for Waterside curlers to resort to that quiet little stream, the Luggie, which poor David Gray has made classic by his beautiful poem. There are no finer lines in curling literature than those in which the amiable poet describes the ways of the Waterside (Dumbarton) curlers of his day." The poem was written in 1820:

*Now underneath the ice the Luggie growls,*
*And to the polished smoothness curlers come*
*Keenly ambitious. Then for happy hours*
*The clinking stones are slid from wary hands,*
*And Barleycorn, best wine for surly airs,*
*Bites i' th' mouth, and ancient jokes are crack'd.*
*And oh, the journey homeward, when the sun,*
*Low-rounding to the west, in ruddy glow*
*Sinks large, and all the amber-skirted clouds,*
*His flaming retinue, with dark'ning glow*
*Diverge! The broom is brandished as the sign*
*Of conquest, and impetuously they boast*
*Of how this shot was played—with what a bend*
*Peculiar—the perfection of all art—*
*That stone came rolling grandly to the Tee*
*With victory crowned, and flinging wide the rest*
*In lordly crash! Within the village inn,*
*What time the stars are sown in ether keen,*
*Clear and acute with brightness; and the moon*
*Sharpens her semicircle; and the air*
*With bleakly shivering sough cuts like a scythe,*
*They by the roaring chimney sit and quaff*
*The beaded "Usqueba" with sugar dash'd.*
*Oh when the precious liquid fires the brain*
*To joy, and every heart beats fast with mirth*
*And ancient fellowship, what nervy grasps*
*Of horny hands o'er tables of rough oak!*

*What singing of "Lang Syne" till teardrops shine*
*And friendships brighten as the evening wanes!*

Rated as "by far the worthiest successor of the famous Kirkcudbright poet Davidson" in the matter of writing poems on the game of curling in the early nineteenth century, "was the minister of Balmaclellan and laird of Troquhain— the Rev. George Murray, who began . . . to celebrate in song his love of the game and the deeds of his curling compeers." It was during the transition period when curling stones were in the process of becoming the product of skilled handiwork rather than being as nature alone had formed them. The following lines were written in praise of his modernized channel-stone which he had named "The Dean", in honour of Dean Swift. He describes the finding of stones in nature's setting, and then their re-shaping and fitting:

*Where lone Penkiln, mid foam and spray*
*O'er many a linn leaps on his way,*
*A thousand years and mair ye lay*
  *Far out of sight:*
*My blessings on the blythesome day*
  *Brought thee to light.*

*Though ye were slippery as an eel,*
*Rab fished ye frae the salmon wiel,*
*And on his back the brawny chiel*
  *Has ta'en ye hame,*
*Destined to figure at the spiel*
  *And roaring game.*

*Wi' mony a crack he cloured your croun,*
*Wi' mony a chap he chipped ye down*
*Fu' aft he turned ye roun' and roun',*
  *And aye he sang*
*A' ither stanes ye'll be aboon*
  *And that ere lang.*

*Guided by many a mould and line*
*He laboured next with polish fine,*
*To make your mirrored surface shine*
  *With lustre rare—*

Like lake, reflect the forms divine
        Of nature fair.

A handle next did Rab prepare,
And fixed it with consummate care—
The wood of ebony so rare,
        The screw of steel—
Ye were a channel-stane right fair,
        Fit for a spiel.

Ye had nae name for icy war—
Nae strange device, nor crest, nor star—
Only a thread of silver spar
        Ran through your blue;
Ilk curler kenned your flinty scar
        And running true.

A time will come when I no more
May fling thee free from shore to shore;
With saddened heart I'll hand thee o'er
        To some brave chiel,
That future times may hear thy roar
        At ilka spiel.

At Lochwinnoch in 1850 a Grand Match was held between representative curlers from the north and south of the Clyde. Some misunderstanding arose whereby the curlers were denied the use of the famous Loch, where they had expected to play. So Colonel M'Dowall of Garthland, living up to the tradition of his famous curling sire, flooded 20 acres of Barr Meadow for them, the match being played there January 11th, with no less than 127 rinks on each side. This notable gathering, the largest of its kind till then, was given a fine memorial in the following verses by Principal Shairp, a famous Scottish poet of the time, and principal of St. Andrews University:

## THE LOCHWINNOCH BONSPIEL

Cauld and snell is the weather, ye curlers, come gather!
Scotland summons her best frae the Tweed to the Tay;

*It's the North o' the Clyde 'gainst the Southern side,*
*And Lochwinnoch the tryst for our Bonspiel today.*

*Ilk parish they've summoned baith landward and borough,*
*Far and near troop the lads wi' the stanes and the broom;*
*The ploughs o' the Loudons stand stiff in the furrow,*
*And the weavers o' Beith for the loch leave the loom.*

*The braw shepherd lads they are there in their plaids,*
*Their hirsels they've left on the Tweedside their lane.*
*Grey carles frae the moorlands wi' gleg e'e and sure hands,*
*Braid bonnet o' blue, and the big channel-stane.*

*And the Loudons three, they foregather in glee,*
*Wi' tounsfolk frae Ayr, and wi' farmers on Doon,*
*Out over the Forth come the men of the North,*
*Frae the far Athole braes, and the palace o' Scone.*

*Auld Reekie's top sawyers, the lang-headed lawyers,*
*And crouse Glasgow merchants are loud i' the play;*
*There are lairds frae the east, there are lords frae the west,*
*For the peer and the ploughman are marrows to-day.*

*See the rinks are a' marshalled, how cheery they mingle,*
*Blithe callants, stout chiels, auld grey-headed men;*
*And the roar o' their stanes gars the snowy heights tingle*
*As they ne'er did before, and may never again.*

*Some lie at hog score, some o'er tha' ice roar;*
*"Here's the tee", "There's the winner", "Chap and lift him twa yards";*
*"Lay a guard", "Fill the port", and now there's nocht for't*
*But a canny inwick or a rub at the guards.*

*Gloamin' comes; we maun pairt; but fair fa' ilk kind heart,*
*Wi' the auld Scottish blood beating warm in his veins;*
*Curlers! aye we've been leal to our country's weal,*
*Though our broadswords are besoms, our targes are stanes.*

A match had been held at Linlithgow two years before
when, it is recorded, six thousand curlers and spectators
were present. Both meetings provide evidence that by the
middle of the nineteenth century curling had become recognized as the national game of Scotland. The very best repre-

sentatives of Scottish manhood are said either to have taken
part in, or been spectators of, those gigantic spiels.

The last of these Scottish curling poems has been selected because it can be sung to the tune of *Auld Lang Syne*,
a tune long familiar to all the English-speaking world.

### THE CURLER'S GRIP

*Losh, man! I'm glad to see yoursel'.*
*I'm glad to meet a freen';*
*But, man, the pleasure's greater still*
*When he's a curler keen.*

*Sae gie's the curler's grip, my freen',*
*Sae gie's the curler's grip.*
*Losh man! I'm glad to see yoursel',*
*Sae gie's the curler's grip.*

*We've played thegither mony a time*
*Around the curlin' tee;*
*I've sooped ye aften up the ice,*
*You've dune the same to me.*

*Sae gie's the curler's grip, my freen',*
*Sae gie's the curler's grip.*
*Losh man! I'm glad to see yoursel',*
*Sae gie's the curler's grip.*

*Man! when I feel a grip like that,*
*I'm unca sweir'd to part;*
*The blood rins din'lin up my arm*
*And warms my very heart.*

*Sae gie's the curler's grip, my freen',*
*Sae gie's the curler's grip.*
*Losh man! I'm glad to see yoursel',*
*Sae gie's the curler's grip.*

*But as the nicht is gye weel thro',*
*Let's hae anither nip,*
*And drink success to ilka ane*
*That kens the curler's grip.*

*Sae gie's the curler's grip, my freen',*
*Sae gie's the curler's grip.*
*Losh man! I'm glad to see yoursel',*
*Sae gie's the curler's grip.*

In the poetic selections that have to do with Canada's love of curling we are fortunate in securing two which were composed as tributes of welcome to that pioneer band in transatlantic curling which, by its visit to North America, probably did more to endear Scotland to Canada than could a group of high government officials or diplomats have done. In fact, a welcome such as had been accorded no other group of men who have come to us was given those Scottish brooms-men when they visited us in the 1902-1903 curling season. They were welcomed and entertained everywhere from Halifax to Vancouver, while their welcome in the United States was equally as warm.

Taking the two selections in order of their publication we find the verses of welcome composed by Mrs. William McNab of Halifax come first:

### WELCOME

*A thousand welcomes and a thousand more*
*To this new land—our grand Canadian shore;*
*You're brother curlers all! A welcome true*
*And hearty we extend to you.*

*Our land is all before you, from the open door*
*At Halifax.—A thousand welcomes more*
*Will greet you all along the snowy way;*
*New friends and hearty cheer from day to day.*

*Some call our land "The Lady of the Snows",*
*But 'tis in truth the Kingdom of the Rose.*
*Would you could see it in the early Spring,*
*When ice melts, flowers bloom, and sweet birds sing.*

*Or in the rich warm, glowing summer time,*
*When fragrant flowers and fruit are in their prime;*

Or in the autumn, when the vast wheat fields,
The vines and orchards, each their harvest yields.

From ocean far across to ocean grand,
It is a goodly, fair and pleasant land;
To it we bid you welcome, Scotchmen true;
We'll do the very best we can for you.

E'en though it be we're nae Tam Samson's bairns,
Yet well we love old Scotland's vales and cairns,
Her mountains, lochs and glens, her purple heather,
The plaidie, bonnet blue, the kilt and feather.

Noo play the game wi' brooms and stanes and a',
Play me ane there wi' jist a canny draw;
And gin ye find ye're sometimes sorely pressed,
Play elbow out or in as ye think best.

Oh hey! for Scotland's dear and bonny name;
Oh hey! the pleasures o' the roarin' game.
Shout, curlers! make the very welkin ring—
"Scotland forever" and "God Save the King".

The second Canadian welcome in verse was composed by a true poet of curling from the great curling Province of Ontario:

## A CORDIAL WELCOME

Thrice welcome to our curling friends
    From ancient Scotia's shore,
Where first the channel-stanes were played
    On winter's icy floor.

They've left their worldly cares behind,
    And crossed the heav'ng sea
To curl against their curling sons
    In Canada the free.

They curl on ponds, 'mid upland muirs,
    Exposed to wind and weather,
Where waups and muirfowl shelter find
    Among the gorse and heather.

*Though wintry winds bring drifting snow,*
*Or blasts of plashing rain,*
*They still play on and face the storm*
*With undisguised disdain.*

*Till night has blotted daylight out*
*They play the manly game,*
*Their guerdon bracing exercise,*
*And glorious curling fame.*

*We play in large capacious rinks,*
*Shielded from every blast,*
*Nor fear the low'ring, threat'ning sky,*
*With rain or snow o'er-cast.*

*Nor do we fear the day's decline,*
*Nor dread the coming night,*
*We've stored up electricity*
*To flood the rink with light.*

*Our Seasons march in order due,*
*Spring, summer, fall and winter;*
*None come too soon, none linger on*
*The season next to hinder.*

*Then welcome to our Scottish friends,*
*We'll play the game together;*
*We'll learn from them, they'll learn from us,*
*We're birds of the same feather.*

J. S. R.

The three selections which follow are of my own making. The first one deals not with the welcoming of Scottish curlers to Canada, but with the welcoming home of one of the members of the Sydney Curling Club on his return from Scotland where he had been a member of a carefully chosen band of curlers who had gone overseas during the winter of 1920-1. Our man, John, had pulled his weight and perhaps a shade more in the many games in which he had taken part in the Old Land; and so we had thought it only fitting that a beef and greens dinner, followed by a welcoming programme, should be given in his honour.

### OOR JOHNNY'S BACK HOME AGAIN

There are heroes of ours who fought to the Rhine
And drove the gray Boche from the Hindenburg Line,
      Leaving homeland and kindred and all.
To the War of the World we sent many a lad
Who routed the foemen from Mons to Bagdad
      Or died with their backs to the wall.

But tonight—though we honour the helmet and plume—
We turn to the lads o' the bonnet and broom
      Who in Scotland their brithers did meet,
And won for their ain land true glory and fame
As they shot from the hack in the auld Scottish game
      'Neath the shadows of grim Arthur's seat.

There, I'm told, 'twas reported in mony Scotch dailies
How oor John brawly lickit some provosts and bailies—
      E'en won against far bigger men:
For dootless he skipped some graund games in top form
'Gainst the Duke o' Montrose or the Marquis o' Lorne,
      Or p'raps whuppit the Laird o' Cockpen.

He was welcomed and greeted on every side
By men frae the Forth to the banks o' the Clyde,
      Ilka ane a genuine Scot.
In their rinks at the games he met "Mac's" by the score,
And Campbells and Gordons and sic like galore—
      Not an English John Bull in the lot.

Noo hae ye e'er seen a mon take a quart frae his hip,
Strip off the tin-foil, wind a screw thru' the tip,
      Then fix it vise-fast twixt his knees,
While a' in rapt silence awaiting the end
See the broad shoulders stiffen, the elbow upbend,
      As he pulls the cork out by degrees?

Well John here saw that in the land o' Prince Charlie:
Saw the glasses brim o'er wi' the cream o' the barley—
      Glenlivet, Scotch Dew, or Black Label.
Yet amid a' their quaffin' I ha nae a doot
That oor mon on cauld water sat every Scot oot
      Or saw them slide under the table.

*For nae tippler is John. He'd gude halesome farin'*
*On parritch, Scotch Haggis, or braw callar herrin'—*
*Every dish for which Reekie is famed.*
*Yet in spite o' sic care wi' his drinkin' and eatin',*
*There were times more than twa when oor hero was beatin';*
*But we all know that John can explain.*

The wee sprite frae the air—the little unseen Queen of Curling—forms the subject of my second contribution. She took her recognized place in the game about a century ago. Somewhere in the mystic region of Elfland she had, in essence, existed, until the tense spirit of some desperate curler away off in Scotland called on her for guidance. Although her fame is auld, her youth is eternal, and her powers are so great that she can serve curlers in all parts of the world, simultaneously. She was represented at first as a maiden, tall and graceful, swaying with an airy balance a-top of THE GRIP. Yet to us she persists in appearing as a cute, jaunty wean.

## THE SPIRIT O' CURLING

On the sheen o' THE GRIP a wee sprite frae the air
Rides awa doun THE ICE wi' her heart a' aflame;
In the path o' the wind gleams the gowd o' her hair—
Wha is SHE? Mon, Mon, she's THE SOUL O' THE GAME.

She sways and she swings on her gossamer wings,
Her twa een intent on the braw arms that SWEEP
Fore the front o' THE STANE as it enters THE RINGS
Thru' a narra bit PORT like a ship frae the deep.

She kens ilka laddie o' CURLING maun learn
How to play on THE BROOM wi' the hand and the ee;
How to lay doun A GUARD wi' an OOT—or IN—TURN;
How to WICK and curl in on the face o' THE TEE.

*In a rollicking mood the spunkie wean stands*
*On her curling ROCK speeding anither to greet;*
*Tho' THE CHAPPIN' ha hurled her a' doun on her hands,*
*In a twinkling she's back on the tips o' her feet.*

*Her youth is eternal, auld auld is her fame;*
*She's lithesome, she's bonnie, she's canty, she's gleg;*
*She lo'es ilka move that belongs to THE GAME,*
*Frae plain KNOCKIN' OOT to CRACKIN' AN EGG.*

*So toast HER ye sons o' THE STANE and THE BROOM!*
*She's a poem in motion, as swaying and whirling*
*She rides on undaunted to victory or doom*
*THE VERRA SOUL O' THE GAME, THE SPIRIT O' CURLING.*

And here is my final contribution:

## THE STORY AND THE GLORY O' CURLING

*Of a' the rare glories which Scotland can boast*
*May her GAME O' THE ICE, my dear Mon, be a toast*
*While memory its power retains;*
*For her bonneted sons where the wild heather blooms*
*Frae the first o' the land are a' knights o' the brooms;*
*And they stand to a man by THE STANES.*

*Frae her ponds and her lochs this auld game has spread*
*To whauriver the men o' The Tartans are bred*
*And in time will be under a' flags.*
*For in lands o' the world wheniver folk gather*
*There are those whose forebears in yon land o' the heather*
*Hae played wi' THE STANES frae the crags.*

*For frae Caledon's crags—grim walls of the Main—*
*Comes the rough rugged block o' the hard granite stane*
*To be fashioned on outlines sae planned*
*That when placed on the ice on its keen nether ring*
*A dead rock then becomes sae wondrous a thing*
*As to live at the touch of a hand.*

*And this game that was born in far days o' lang syne*
*Is a power to-day in your land and mine,*
*Whaur men are sae kittle and free*
*That twa curlers may clash in fierce party debate,*
*Or damn ane anither o'er matters of State,*
*Who'll shake honds in the rings o' the TEE.*

*Ah I fain would believe—to all hearts that are pure—*
*That the game we a' love will forever endure;*
*That e'en mem'ries aboot it may steal*
*Through the souls o' past curlers in that happy beyond*
*Whaur men dinna forget, and whaur hond may grip hond*
*In that wonderfu' Land o' The Leal.*

*So a toast to THE GAME, let its praises be sung*
*As year follows year, by auld men and young,*
*By our sweethearts and wives who hae curled!*
*Let's aye drink to a sport that is worthy o' Kings—*
*The game o' the frost lands, the ice lands, THE RINGS,*
*Till her STANES rumble a' roun' the world.*

The following verses appeared in the *North American Curling News*:

### THE CURLER SPEAKS

O the squash men thrill
To the lightning kill,
Or the shot that dies by the wall;
And the ski-er yearns
For telemark turns
And for slaloms with never a fall.

The crash of the pins
And the strike that wins
To the bowler are sweeter than honey;
And the hockey fan dreams
Of the gallery's screams
And the puck in the cage for money.

There's the smack of a drive,
And a sloop that's alive
And hands on a hunter's withers;
In sporting lore
There are thrills by the score,—
But they all seem tame to "The Brithers."

Give me the drone
Of a running stone,
"On the broom" and curling free;
Or a shot laid hard
To take out a guard,
Or a draw through a port to the tee.

And "SWEEP!" from the lip
Of a salty skip
Or "Don't be narrow or light—
Just let her bend
And we'll take the end";
Now "SWEEP! You can make her bite."

The potent kick
Of a chap or a wick
Must be felt to be understood;
Or a stone well laid
And a shot that's played
So it comes to rest where it should.

*Be a slave to your sports*
*That are played in courts*
*Or on alleys or fields say I.*
*YOU'LL be paroled*
*When you get too old;*
*But I'LL curl till the day I die.*

*And as springtime looms*
*And we stack the brooms*
*And lift the stones to the rack;*
*I'll sigh for the time*
*When the ice is prime*
*And my toe's once more on the hack.*

—STUART PEABODY,
Ardsley Curling Club

To conclude, here is an old curling rhyme in which curling is represented not as a godsend in a figurative sense only, but a godsend in actual fact and deed. In other words it is claimed that curling is a gift to us, straight from the heavens above! As this amazing account of the origin of the game is in direct contradiction to the account given in another chapter, I thought it only fair to present it here:

## AULD DADDY SCOTLAND

*Auld Daddy Scotland sat ae day*
*Bare leggit on a snawy brae,*
*His brawny arms wi' cauld were blae,*
    *The wind was snelly blawing:*
*As icicles froze at his snout.*
*He rowed his plaid his head about,*
*Syne raired to heaven a roupit shout,*
    *Auld Albyn's Jove misca'ing:*

Chorus:
    *Oh! for a cheery, heartsome game,*
    *To send through a' the soul a flame,*
    *Pitt birr and smeddum in the frame,*
        *And set the blude a-din'ling.*

Oh, dool and wae! This wretched clime!
What care I for our hills sublime
If covered aye wi' frosty rime?
    I'm right mischantlie dealt wi'
Quo' Jove, and gied his kilt a heeze,
"Fule carle! what gars you grunt and wheeze?
Get up! I'll get an exercise
    To het your freezing pelt wi'."

Chorus:
    I'll get a cheery, heartsome game,
    To send through a' the soul aflame,
    Pitt birr and smeddum in the frame,
        And set the blude a-din'ling.

Gae, get twa whinstanes, round and hard,
Syne on their taps twa thorn-roots gird,
Then soop the ice for mony a yard,
    And mak' baith tee and colly:
If in the hack your fit ye hide,
And draw or inwick, guard or ride,
Syne wi' your besom after't stride,
    We'll hear no more o' cauld aye.

Chorus:
    That, Sawney, 's what I ca' a game
    To send through a' the soul a flame,
    Pitt birr and smeddum in the frame,
        And set the blude a-din'ling.

*"Great thanks!" auld Daddy Scotland cries,*
*"Sly, pawky chield, for thy advice;"*
*We'll birsle now our shins on ice,*
　　　*Instead o' owre the ingle:*
*Let ilka true-born Scottish son,*
*When cranreuch cleeds the snawy grun',*
*'Mang curling cores seek harmless fun,*
　　　*And gar his heart's blude tingle.*

Chorus:
　　*Oh Curling!  cauld-defying game,*
　　*To send through a' the soul a flame,*
　　*Pitt birr and smeddum in the frame,*
　　　　*And set the blude a-din'ling.*
　　　　　　　　　　　　　OLD SONG

CHAPTER VIII

# CURLING MYSTERIES AND COURTS

*Sae gie's the curler's grip, my freen',*
*Sae gie's the curler's grip.*
*Losh man! I'm glad to see yoursel',*
*Sae gie's the curler's grip.*

OBVIOUSLY, THE SO-CALLED MYSTERIES OF CURLING WILL CEASE
to be mysteries as soon as the initiated start revealing them.
In this materialistic age the serious-minded have, perhaps,
become too literal to give secret signs and pass-words the
respect which, in so many instances, they deserve. And so
it may be concerning the mysterious signs and tokens used by
the members of bygone curling societies. They had—and
should still have—a place, these curling society secrets, if
for no better reason than that "a little nonsense every now
and then is relished by the very best of men."

I have been asked to give in this book an account of all
the fingered signs and whispered words which once upon a
time were so widely used among the Scottish curling fraterni-
ties in all ceremonies having to do with the initiation of new
members. Yet all we or any others can do in the matter of
answering these questions is to pass on to the enquirers what
little has been revealed by such writers on curling as Dr.
Cairnie, Sir Richard Broun or Dr. Kerr. According to such
authorities the mysteries of curling were centred upon THE

115

WORD and THE GRIP. Dr. Cairnie states in his *Essay on Curling* that the Rev. John Witherspoon of Paisley in 1757 became the first to give what is called the "Heigh Linn" curling word. In the account of the formation of the Sanquhar Society in 1774 it transpired that a secret "word" and "grip" had already been in use there; and as an indication of the respective meanings attached, the same was revealed by the following minute adopted by this society at a meeting held two years later:

> Sanquhar, 10th January, 1776.
>
> In order to prevent all disputes concerning the curler "word" and "grip", the master, who always is preses during his office, and the rest of the society, have agreed that the following shall be held reputed the curler word and grip of this society for the future:
>
> The curler word:
>
>> "If you'd be a curler keen,
>> Stand right, look even,
>> Sole well, shoot straight and sweep clean."
>
> The curler grip with explanation:
>
>> Gripping hands in the common manner of shaking hands is the gripping the hand of the curling stone. The little finger of the person examined or instructed thrust in betwixt the thumb and forefinger of the examinator or instructor, signifies "Running a Port". The little finger of the person examined or instructed linked with the little finger of the examinator or instructor, means an "In-Ring".

A Mr. Brown, a one-time historian of the Sanquhar Club, was probably right in supposing that these explanations of "word" and "grip" were only fragmentary and had been taken from far more detailed accounts. In a *Treatise on Curling* issued by the Kilmarnock Club a simpler form of initiation is mentioned as having been a curious old custom in many curling parishes of Perthshire:

> The curler is initiated by receiving the "grip", which consists in catching him by the thumb in the manner that the curling

stone is held, and in making him repeat the curling "word":
"I will fit (fight) fair, sweep well, take all the brittle
(angled) shots I can, and cangle (dispute) to a hair-
breadth".

In The R.C.C.C. *Annual* for 1842 there is an account of
its origin in the well-known Blairgowrie Club:

> In the course of 1782 an inhabitant of Coupar-Angus, "white-
> headed Jamie Cammel", having occasion to be in Edinburgh
> in the prosecution of his trade of cattle-dealer, went out to
> Duddingston Loch to see the play of the south country
> brethren. During the game a very difficult shot occurred, on
> which all the curlers present tried their skill and failed; and
> Mr. Campbell having remarked that he thought he could take
> the shot, was invited to try it and was successful. He after-
> ward continued to play during the day with Duddingston curl-
> ers who were so well pleased with his skill in the game that
> they invited him to dine with them and initiated him a mem-
> ber of the Club by communicating to him the "word" and
> "grip". On his return home to Coupar-Angus he initiated
> members of his own Club from whom the Blairgowrie Club
> received the "sign" and "secret" in the following year.

Note, however, that what *form* this initiation took is
unrevealed. But whatever the form, there was almost bound
to be a general sameness in all these "word" and "grip" ceremonies. Both were confined to the subject of curling and there
would be little chance of some clubs inventing ceremonies
sufficiently original so as not to overlap those of their neighbours. These so-called "mysteries", however few or many of
them there may have been, were used in the main for the purpose of making the person initiated conscious of having become one of a brotherhood and doubtless they were also
looked upon as sources of amusement.

That these "mysteries" were treated with great respect
by some curlers of days gone by is indicated by an entry in
the Hamilton Society record, 1796:

A complaint was made by Robert Pender against Robert Purdie, who gave a new grip to Mr. Sands, one of the new members, never before known to the society; he was accordingly fined of 2s. 6d. to the society and 6d. to the officer, which he refused to pay, and appealed to a general meeting.

The following "mystery" was adopted by the members of the Douglas St. Bride's Club in 1794 as "the correct form":

| Question | Answer |
|---|---|
| 1. Are you a curler? | Keen. |
| 2. What is the duty of a curler? | To behave peaceably and play to direction. |
| 3. What is the greatest pleasure of a curler? | With a good stone on hard ice to defeat his adversary. |

Nix. (Snow)        Gelu. (Frost)        Glacies. (Ice)

*Foot firm and fair,*
*Play to a hair;*
   *Your stone, if well directed,*
*Will hit your aim,*
*And win the game;*
   *If not, be not dejected.*

The foregoing was adopted in an improved form by the oldest of all Canadian Clubs, that formed at Montreal in 1807. Thus we have had the "Mysteries" practised in one club in our "ain Countree". As read in the minute-book of the Montreal Club the words run:

*Foot fair: draw to a hair:*
   *Your stone being well directed,*
*You'll hit your aim, and win the game;*
   *If you miss be not dejected.*

*A Curlers' Court yields fun and sport right from the very start*
*If all of you—not one or two—join in and take a part.*

The practise of a curling club holding a curler's court, is, like Scotland's auld channel-stanes, verra auld. It was first reported as an ancient custom in Perthshire; but its preservation is owing to the Kinross Club, since one of its members went to the trouble of writing out a detailed description of what takes place as it had been passed down by word of mouth from generation to generation. I have personally participated in two of its sessions, yet both were so long ago that I am unable to recall very many details. Here follows the old Kinross record from Dr. Kerr's *History of Curling*:

The first requisite is to elect a President, termed "My Lord"; he is usually the Preses of the Club for the time, but another brother may be chosen. "My Lord" on taking the chair immediately appoints one of the brethren present to be his officer, whom he directs to fence the court. This is done as follows:

A pewter stoup, varying from a mutchkin to a pint (Scottish measure) is procured, which the officer presents to "My Lord"; and he in order to make a noise, drops therein some silver or a few pence, according to his pleasure. The officer, after rattling the money in the stoup three times, and repeating alternately with each shake, "oyez", "oyez", "oyez", fences the court thus: "I defend and I forbid, in His (or Her) Majesty's name and by authority of 'My Lord' presently in the chair— (1) that there shall be no legs o'er em; (2) no hands a-bosy, or across; (3) no supports on your neighbour's chair, or on the table; (4) no private committees; (5) no rising up or sitting down, or going to the door, without leave asked and granted by "My Lord"; (6) no touching the cup or glass but with the curler's right hand, which is understood to be every ordinary man's left; (7) every man his name and surname; (8) every breach of these articles a halfpenny and every oath a penny."

The officer then points out and gives in an audible voice the name and surname of every brother present, commencing on "My Lord's" left hand and going regularly round the whole company thus: "A.B. is A.B.; C.D. is C.D.; E.F. is E.F.; G.H. is G.H.; (and on coming round to "My Lord") "My Lord's 'My Lord' and I am his officer—BOTH ABSOLUTE. God save The King". The officer usually stands opposite to the person named, at the other side of the table, when this can be conveniently done.

If any individuals are present, not yet brethren, as in the case with those to be initiated that evening, the officer passes them over, and these are not subject to the fines and regulations of the court till after initiation.

The proceedings of the court then go on; and it is the special duty of the officer, who remains on his feet, occasionally rattling the stoup, to observe and detect all breaches of the regulations, and to collect the fines in the stoup, rattling it in the ear of the offender until the fine is paid.

The decision of "My Lord", and through him, of his officer in fining, is PERFECTLY ABSOLUTE and must be obeyed. Any one member has a right to report the breaches of another to "My Lord", or to his officer; but if the person complained against conceives himself aggrieved by the report he may protest and appeal, which is done by depositing a penny on the table to be forfeited to the stoup in case of being decided against, which generally happens when an appeal is made. "My Lord" very shortly hears the protestor and gives an absolute decision.

When candidates for the brotherhood are present, "My Lord" (after the court has sat a reasonable time) directs the business of initiation to proceed.

The Candidate, thereupon, respectfully approaches "My Lord", with a curler's besom in his hand, holding it over his right shoulder, and craves to be admitted a member of the honourable court and Club. "My Lord" now appoints ONE of the brethren to give him "THE WORD" and "THE GRIP", and two others (one or both of whom must be masters of the whole secrets), to be reporters as to whether these have been given correctly. The three then conduct the Candidate to an adjoining room which has been previously prepared for the purpose, and after a careful examination that no intruders are present, and shutting the door, the initiation commences by the person appointed by "My Lord" first giving "THE WORD" and then "THE GRIP". If the reporters find that he is unable to give these correctly, they return with him to the court, and report him to "My Lord" as deficient, who immediately appoints some other to the office. The same proceeding is repeated, and appointments made, till a brother is found sufficiently qualified.

"My Lord" often fixes at first on some one to give the secrets whom he suspects to be deficient; and all who fail in this duty are fined, before the closing of the court, at the option of the company—a penny or twopence, or threepence. When a brother is so appointed, he may decline, and come under the mercy of the court, by saying, "I submit"; but he is generally fined in a larger sum than those who make the attempt, but fail.

The reporters, after the Candidate receives the secrets, introduce him to "My Lord" in court, as brother of the broom, and a keen, keen curler. He then goes forward to "My Lord", and holding his hand under the table, out of view, gives "My Lord" THE GRIP; after which he goes to the brother on "My Lord's" left, and holding his hand also below the table, requests that member to give HIM the grip. The newly admitted member must on no account give "THE GRIP" to anyone except "My Lord", but himself receive it; and if the brother, through inattention or otherwise, does not give it to him correctly, he notes the circumstance, and when he has gone round the company in this way (or until "My Lord" says he may stop) he reports to "My Lord" all those who were deficient, and they are fined at the discretion of "My Lord".

When there are more candidates than one, the same proceedings take place with each separately. The court is then fenced anew by the officer, the names of the new brothers being of course included.

During the sitting of the court "My Lord" says, "I give a toast not to be repeated"; and he immediately proposes one, of which he and the other officer keep note, and generally write down for accuracy. Any member who repeats the toast before being specially requested to do so is immediately fined a halfpenny to the stoup. Sometime afterwards, and when the toast may be supposed to be forgotten by many, "My Lord" directs the officer to go round the company and ask each individually what it was: each must whisper it to the officer, so that the person next him cannot hear; if he fails to mention the toast TO THE VERY LETTER, the officer rattles the stoup at his ear, as an intimation that he has failed, and proceeds to the next person, and so on. When he has gone round the whole, he reports to "My Lord" those who failed, and His Lordships directs a fine to be levied from each— generally one penny. Any person conceiving himself aggrieved may protest and appeal in the manner already mentioned.

When "My Lord" thinks that the court has continued a sufficient length of time (usually from half-an-hour to an hour), he directs the officer to "roup the stoup" which is done by him in the character of an auctioneer descanting on the great weight and value of the stoup; offers are made

for the contents in the way of an ordinary auction or roup;
and after it is knocked down to the highest bidder, trifling
bets are sometimes taken as to whether the purchaser has
gained or lost, two reporters being appointed to count the
proceeds in another room. While the reporters are absent
for this purpose, the court goes on, another stoup being used;
and any fines collected during that time, and also during the
roup of the stoup, are added to the original amount, and
belong to the purchaser. "My Lord" then declares the court
closed.

The purchase money is either applied towards defraying the
expense of the social glass, or added to the club funds, according to the general regulations of the club.

It is obvious that as one brother is required for "My Lord",
another for the officer, and three to perform the ceremony
of initiation, the court cannot well proceed unless seven be
present, and this only provides for two sitting in court during
the absence of the initiators; but there is little amusement if
there be not from fifteen to twenty in company.

It is obvious that the programme need never be considered in any way inalterable. There are one or two non-es-
sentials which may be either omitted or changed to meet
conditions militating against carrying out the above schedule
in full. For instance, in a club whose membership runs into
the hundreds, initiation ceremonies—instead of a one by one
process—might be carried on with small selected groups.
And indeed, perhaps with a few additional phrases—whose
omission or alteration would not matter greatly—more suitable arrangements could be agreed upon by each group acting for itself.

At these courts the main source of the fun comes from
the over-eagerness of the younger members, who in their
strong desire to lodge complaints here and there, find themselves caught through not remembering all the warnings
given in, or perhaps through forgetting one of the eight forbidden articles. Over and over again some one of these
curling court youngsters, while impulsively bawling out that
"so-and-so" has one of his legs crossed over the other or

has his hands "a-bosy", will suddenly, and to his surprise and chagrin, hear the stoup rattling in his ear, demanding the instant payment of a fine for having forgotten to ask "My Lord's" leave to rise and speak. As is easily seen the point in all this laugh-producing farce is that these same forbidden body, leg, or hand positions are precisely the natural attitudes which the ordinary mortal sitting with others around a festive board would be most likely to assume.

In my first experience of a curlers' court—being one of five or six waiting to be initiated—we were all blindfolded so as to be made incapable of knowing exactly what was being done to each of us individually. I recall one young unfortunate in that group whose mouth—by carefully drawn charcoal lines — had been greatly lengthened; and thus changed he was made to undergo the further indignity of having this feature explained to a hugely amused gathering as an instance in which the hog line was at long last in its proper place. There was a second unfortunate who, when the blinding muffler had been taken off, beheld himself somewhat untidily arrayed in the unmentionables of the stout old manageress in whose hotel we happened to be celebrating. It was all good fun, anyway.

There are two features, however, in connection with these courts which need to be considered carefully: The first is their frequency. To hold such meetings annually would inevitably result in all members, to whom such gatherings would soon cease to be novelties, becoming too wise to be caught napping in respect to the eight forbidden articles. And the second is the closing of the court a considerable time before the fun begins to lag. "My Lord" and his officer, as the two chief executives, should, if possible, be somewhat of the comedian type seeing that it is their task above all the others to keep the fun going.

Taking these curlers' courts by and large they are, in my humble opinion, assets of such worth in the way of promoting a true spirit of brotherhood that curlers everywhere should think twice before permitting them to die out. To see such great possibilities for enjoyment and good fellowship being refused even a trial or forgotten in places where they had once been regarded as a gala occasion, is not good. If groups of ten clubs, each group within a specified area, could be brought to agree to the holding of curlers' courts with each club taking on once in every ten years, then all involved would be assured of having a sufficient number of the uninitiated class to make this fun-provoking affair a permanent feature in the future world of curling. For these courts, when held at sufficiently long intervals, will show us, as perhaps no other organization in the game, that while we are a' keen, keen curlers, we are also brithers a'.

# PART TWO

# Curling in North America

CHAPTER I

# CURLING IN EASTERN CANADA

*Whauriver Scotland's curling sons have gone,*
*We're tauld their stanes frae time to time went too;*
*And when enow was had to live upon,*
*Amang them a' up sprang the game anew.*

## Nova Scotia

Nova Scotia's first curling club was formed in Halifax in
the winter of 1824-5 when the small seaside settlement could
boast of only seventy-five years of existence. Three men
who took the lead in this first stage of curling in Nova Scotia
were Captain (afterwards known as Admiral Sir Houston)
Stewart, Colonel Graeg and Dr. Grigor. This Halifax organization was in fact not only the first curling club, but for a
number of years, the only one in the province. In time, others
began one by one to make their appearance. In 1773, just
twenty-four years after the founding of Halifax, a little immi-
grant ship called the *Hector* had dropped anchor in the
harbour of Pictou on the northern coast of Nova Scotia. Her
passengers to the last soul were decidedly of the persuasion
of John Knox. These home-seeking immigrants, on leaving
the Old Country for the unknown wilds of the New, had
sterner matters to think about than whether curling stones
had been stowed away in the hold of the *Hector*. They must
have realized that their remaining years would be almost

wholly taken up in the erecting of homes and the clearing of land. In fact, neither they nor those immediately succeeding them were destined to become the pioneer curlers in and around the little settlement of Pictou. For in 1829 the discovery of coal in the vicinity of New Glasgow resulted in a number of miners being sent out from Scotland and these miners, report has it, brought their stanes with them and played the winter seasons in a flooded hollow near the pit's mouth.

The first notable contest in which Pictou curlers had a part occurred in 1851, when clubs from Halifax and Pictou were opponents in a whole day's curling match on the ice of a millpond two miles from Truro. Both clubs played three rinks with five men a side; two thousand spectators from near and far stood looking on; and when the day closed they all assembled at the Prince of Wales hotel where, when keen appetites had been satisfied, speeches and songs followed in rapid succession until the friendly opponents parted company in the wee sma' hours, the Halifax men having to drive sixty-two miles and the Pictou men forty-two.

According to the records of the Nova Scotia Branch, the clubs of both Halifax and Pictou became affiliated with the R.C.C.C. in 1852. Then there came a succession of clubs. The Bluenose of New Glasgow came into being in 1853. Rinks probably belonging to the second generation of this club gained the unique distinction of winning at Ottawa the Governor-General's Gold Medal four years in succession. Following the Bluenose we have the Cape Breton Club of North Sydney in 1863, the Truro Club in 1875, the Sydney Club in 1877, and the Antigonish Club in 1884. The events that led to the formation of these clubs are not recorded save in the cases of North Sydney and Sydney. Two brothers, named Purvis, who had migrated from Pictou to the north side of Sydney harbour in the fifties, were in later years instrumental in the forming of a curling club at North Sydney, further up the coast; and nine years later the Northside curlers gave aid in turn to their neighbours across the harbour in the formation of a second Island club. Both clubs are flourishing today, the latter possessing a four-sheet artifical-ice rink.

During the final years of the last century and the early years of the present, five more clubs were formed—Stellarton, Amherst, the Halifax Mayflowers, Yarmouth, and Westville. Nova Scotia today has twenty-three curling clubs.

## New Brunswick

On the 24th December, 1854, in Fredericton, curling was given its start in the United Empire Loyalist Province of New Brunswick. The story of how that pioneer club came to be organized is told by the founder himself in a letter addressed to the club president in 1883:

Gibson, Feb. 6, 1883.

Mr. President and Gentlemen of the
Fredericton Curling Club:

It is nearly 30 years since this club was first organized— December 24th, 1854, 19 years of which I was an active member and keen curler, but since I retired from business and settled on my farm at Gibson, I have only (through your kindness) been an honorary member, though it is unnecessary for me to say how deeply I feel interested in promoting the success of the club; and in order to encourage emulation in the noble game of curling, I beg leave to present the club with this silver rink medal, to be competed for annually in matches as you may think proper.

When curling was started here we had never heard of it in any part of North America. One day the late Mr. Ludlow Robinson came into my store and threw down a Glasgow *Herald* to me at the desk, saying, "Neill, what sort of a game is this curling? Here is a description of a great match in Scotland filling six columns of this large paper. Could you not start it here?"

I immediately commenced reading the paper and got quite enthusiastic over it, and at once started with a paper to get subscribers for a curling club and I offered to import the stones. I tried all over Fredericton and could only get the following seven names: Robert Fulton, John Taylor, Robert Thornburn, William McLean, Alexander McKilligan, Barry Phair and James Moore. They only subscribed for one stone each, not knowing whether it would be a success here or not. Next year we got a *pair*. I then imported two dozen pairs of curling stones (in some parts of Scotland they are called channel-stones; mostly in the south). When they landed in St. John the custom house officials did not know what to make of them. The nearest they could guess was shoemakers' lap-stones. They wrote up to me to know what they were, and I sent them the invoice. At the Crystal Palace exhibit in London the cockneys thought they were models for cheeses.

We had great difficuty at first in getting good ice. We tried the river, Heron's Lake and the Naskwaak and several other places, but never had so good a place as we got at last in the officers' square. We petitioned the Colonel of the regiment and got it on condition that we would make our rinks on the gravelled road and not on the grass. We then had to haul the water in casks on sleds, which was very laborious work. We sank a well outside the fence, intending to pump the water on the rink, but went into a deep bed of clay, and could get no water.

It takes a vast deal of energy and perseverance to establish a club, and hoping that this rink medal will go down to future generations as an historical memento of the first formation of the club, I remain, gentlemen,

Yours very truly,

JOHN NEILL.

P.S. Lord Eglinton once mentioned in a letter to the Ayrshire curlers that he attached great importance to curling as the medium of bringing together all classes of the community in a friendly spirit of competition. On the ice it is not what you are but what you can do. If the Marquis of Lorne misses it and you—plain Sandy—take it out, the Marquis of Lorne, Governor-General of Canada, is nowhere alongside of you on the ice. J.N.

On the occasion of John Neill's death in 1893, the *Daily Gleaner* of Fredericton concluded its account of his long, useful life in these words: "Mr. Neill was a Scotchman born and bred in 'The Auld Countree' and a most worthy and honourable representative of that noble race."

Curling in the Province of New Brunswick must have made solid progress in those early days, seeing that in 1869 a match was played between the "Home-Born Scots" and the "Native-Born" with the N.B.'s coming out as the victors; and not long afterwards the records tell of another match somewhat on the Scottish Lochwinnoch plan of North against South, but as to the result the records are silent.

Thus, from the times of these contests it can be seen that the Fredericton Club was soon followed by others. The first of these was the St. Andrews Club of Saint John, in 1855. The Thistle Club of the same city, along with Bathurst, Chatham, Newcastle, Moncton and Campbellton, came later but have each, nonetheless, given ample evidence that their players must be taken seriously.

Mr. R. T. Bennett, secretary of the Moncton Curlers' Association, gives the following resumé of local curling activity:

> In the past seven years the number of curlers in Moncton has grown from less than 100 to over 500. A second club has been established (the Beaver Curling Club). The original club (our own club) now has 280 active members, and the Beaver Club must have well over 250. Our club has torn down the old club house and built a new one. We have added a fourth sheet of ice. We have remodelled the rink, inside and out, and have put in an artificial-ice plant. High school curling is in effect, and the High School Provincial Bonspiel was held at our rink last winter. This season the provincial bonspiel will be held at Moncton.

## NEWFOUNDLAND

The third curling province on the Atlantic side of Canada is Newfoundland, which has long been regarded by the peoples of the Maritimes as one of themselves. And though this rugged isle of fogs and storms may not be possessed of a superabundance of curlers, those who follow the game have repeatedly shown themselves to be both keen and skilful, as I can truly testify.

Their first club, the Avalon, was organized by a group of Scots in St. John's in 1843. Throughout a long period their curling was carried on under the open sky until they finally succeeded in the erection of a spacious rink in 1869 at the not inconsiderable cost of £2,000. In 1874 they were given medals for competitive play by the R.C.C.C., and this thoughtful contribution had the happy result of greatly increasing the local interest in the game. Not only did a second St. John's Club, the Arctic, come into being in the following year, but in 1878 a third club was organized at Heart's Content on the western side of Conception Bay. Six years later two additional clubs were formed in St. John's, but four rinks soon proved too many for the one centre. All amalgamated in 1885 under the name of the St. John's Curling Club. Heart's Content after an existence of only a few years was compelled to drop out of the game, but the Bell Island Club was formed in 1915 and industrial Corner Brook broke into the picture in the winter of 1944. The curlers of St. John's, prevented by a succession of non-frosty winters from enjoying their game, were driven to install a freezing plant in 1938. Three years later the old rink and its new plant went up in smoke; but the valiant curlers were so truly the decendants of their forebears of 1869 that by 1943 they had not only erected another building with special accommodation for the ladies but had also installed a second freezing plant sufficient for four sheets of ice. The new building was formally opened on 24th January, 1943. The St. John's Curling Club, incorporated in 1941, is now known as the St. John's Curling Association, Ltd.

Those Newfoundland curlers are so hospitable that they carry the very spirit of curling with them on trips abroad. At the close of the sixth end in a match we played against them in Sydney, every Newfoundland man dropped his broom with a shout of "Barleycorn! Barleycorn!" and this somewhat suspicious word was soon given a true "barley" meaning in our assembly room when they invited all and sundry to partake of a concoction that "bites i' the mouth."

## PRINCE EDWARD ISLAND

Curling in Prince Edward Island began in the capital city of Charlottetown in 1887. The Charlottetown Curling Club had an original strength of thirty-six members, and began curling activities by leasing its playing periods from skating rinks. In 1913 a curling rink was built on lower Grafton Street, but it was not until after 1919 that a satisfactory increase in membership was secured. In 1938 the club moved to a new rink on Euston Street, with comfortable social quarters in connection. The Province's representation in the Dominion Curling Playdowns in 1936 gave a great stimulus to the game, and both membership and interest greatly increased. At the beginning of 1948 the club installed an up-to-date artificial-ice plant for its four sheets, and has now approximately 200 playing members besides a number of associate members.

The Montague Curling Club was organized in January, 1927, with a membership of twenty-four. The first curling rink was a one-sheet ice surface building attached to the skating rink. It served its purpose well, and Montague has always been represented by rinks of high standing in the various provincial curling competitions. In 1936 the club made a clean sweep of major events, winning the Mac-Arthur, Gaboury and British Consols Trophies. In the following years the membership greatly increased, and in March, 1944, it was decided to build on the grounds of the Community Welfare League. The rink today, of wooden structure, has a two-sheet ice surface. In 1945 the Ladies' Auxiliary of the hospital added a large kitchen to the premises, and Montague boasts a club par excellence where hospitality to all visiting rinks is the keynote.

Curling was introduced in Alberton through the efforts of the late W. P. Keenan, formerly a resident of Fredericton, N.B. In December, 1937, the Alberton Curling Club was formed, and regular games were played that season, with seven teams in competition, on a one-rink sheet of ice attached to the side of a new skating rink. The club progressed slowly until the winter of 1946-7 when the membership grew to forty members. During the summer of 1947 a new rink was built, providing two sheets of ice.

The Summerside Curling Club was organized in 1926. It purchased the old Crystal Skating Rink, which was its home until 1948 when work began on a new rink. This has recently been completed, at a cost of about $55,000. The building has three sheets of artificial ice and excellent accommodation for social activities. Delays in the installation of the freezing equipment inevitably occurred, but curling finally began in January, 1949. The men's curling membership jumped from its low of forty in 1948 to 180; fifty-three lady curlers and seventy-nine school boys were also enrolled. The club is the first in the province to inaugurate membership for ladies and is also one of the first in Eastern Canada to introduce curling for boys.

These four clubs—the Charlottetown, Montague, Alberton and Summerside—are linked in the Provincial Association, which was organized in 1934. In 1936, and in each successive year, the association has been represented by a provincial rink in the Dominion Curling Playdowns. Besides the provincial championship, which confers the right to represent the province in the Playdowns, the Prince Edward Island Curling Association conducts a number of other interclub competitions. In 1947 the association inaugurated also the Confederation Bonspiel, an invitation bonspiel primarily for the Maritimes but open to all curling-club members in good standing. In the first two years, competitors were entered from Ontario, Quebec and Newfoundland in addition to the three Maritime provinces. Approximately one half of the contestants are Prince Edward Island curlers, who are thus gaining an opportunity to meet large numbers of visitors both in the curling contests and in the attendant social activities of the week.

## QUEBEC

The Quebec City Curling Club was founded in 1821, but it can safely be assumed that the sick and wounded of Fraser's Regiment, or the Seventy-Eighth Highlanders who fought at Ste. Foy under General Murray in 1760, curled on the ice of the St. Charles River during the days of their convalescence. The Quebec Club, until the building in 1867 of the first indoor rink, a low wooden structure on St. Charles Street, played the "roarin' game" in the open air, on the famous Plains of Abraham, the Cove Fields, on the St. Lawrence when a smooth ice bridge formed, on the St. Charles near the Gillespie and Bell farms, and on several wharves of the Lower Town.

Games were also played by the Quebec curlers at Three Rivers, Berthier-en-Haut, Montreal, and even as far as Kingston at a time when they were obliged to drive the entire distance. The rink building in Montreal where the Quebec men played several matches in 1840 was located in that area, near the water front, which is known as Griffintown. The defeated team in those days generally paid for a dinner at a cost that must have had a sobering effect. It is recorded that one of the Montreal clubs had a rule that the losing party of the day must pay for a bowl of whiskey toddy to be placed in the middle of the table for all who might wish to partake.

The Quebec City Curling Club has on its rolls some distinguished names: the Earl of Dalhousie, Governor of Canada, was a member in 1828. Lord Dufferin, who was a patron, played his first game in Canada on the ice of this club in 1873; and one of the club's most valuable trophies is a cup wrought in Scotland in 1723, a gift from the Marquis of Lorne, Governor-General in 1878. The charter members of 1821 were Messrs. Andrew Paterson, Robert Paterson, Andrew Weir, William Findlay, A. Moir, William Pemberton, M. McKenzie, William Phillips, L. P. MacPherson, J. C. MacTavish, James G. Heath, George Pemberton and Thomas Greegan. At one period in the club's history none save Scots were admitted to membership, but such an exclusive ruling has long been abandoned.

The Quebec Club was incorporated by an Act of the Legislature in 1868. As one of the many additional clubs that Quebec curlers have organized in recent years the Etchemin is well worthy of note. It was brought into being in 1935 by a small group of English- and French-Canadians at St. Romauld d'Etchemin on the southern shore of the harbour of Quebec, ten miles west of the city. This club has not only promoted the game of curling but has also made a marked contribution to the *bonne entente* between the two races inhabiting Quebec.

Fig. 48

Nearly all of Quebec's better known Curling organizations, great or small, are in the south-western part of the province between the City of Quebec and the line of the

Ottawa river. Montreal with its teeming population takes the lead not only as the chief curling city of its own province but as one of the two leading curling cities in Eastern Canada. The Royal Montreal, founded in 1807, is the oldest curling club in North America. The curlers of Montreal are the only followers of the game who, on the ground that more scientific play is possible, have taken to the use of irons.

Mr. William Brown of the Granite Curling Association, Montreal has contributed the following in respect to the use of irons in the Province of Quebec:

> The use of irons originated in the City of Quebec, at the time of its capture by the British, since many of the troops were looking for the opportunity of participating in a game to which they had been accustomed in the Old Country, but, naturally, under the then prevailing circumstances, importation of granites was impossible, and some one conceived the idea of melting down cannon balls and providing a narrow running surface, and, since then, the greater portion of our play has been with irons. Originally, these weighed between 56 and 64 lbs., and until some few years ago, because of the variation in the running surface, the irons were moved from rink to rink, which entailed considerable expense. For many years these have been made from cast iron, the metal being run into a mould, and the running surface polished, and since they run on a wider edge than granites, they take a lesser borrow. Some few years ago the idea of standardizing the weight and shape of irons was conceived, and, as a result, the owners of the irons donated them to their several clubs, by whom they were turned over to the manufacturer, who converted them to a standard measurement and weight of 58½ lbs., thus dispensing with the necessity of cartage, and establishing a uniformity in size and weight which has proved very beneficial to the game as a whole. In later years granites have grown in popularity, in spite of the claim by the older generation that the iron game is superior in many respects to the granites, but there is evidence on many hands that before very long, the curlers of Quebec Province will confine their play to granites, so as to establish uniformity throughout Canada, and place the curlers of this province on a parity with the curlers of the other provinces. Another strong argument in favour of this anticipated change is to be

found in the fact that it would prolong the life of the average curler, since the continuance of play, after he reaches the age of seventy, with irons weighing some 60 lbs., is not to be recommended, and often bars players from active participation in the game.

Conditions under which the game is now carried on, both in Quebec and in other pioneer curling provinces of Canada, differ in some marked respects from those of former days. The annual bonspiels, now housed in massive rink buildings, may perhaps be more impressive than were the old out-of-door gatherings, but whether they are more exciting may well be doubted. The illustrations of an open air match in a bonspiel held in the long ago on the ice of the St. Lawrence (Fig. 48), the opening of the Caledonia Rink in Montreal in 1869 by H.R.H. Prince Arthur of Connaught (Fig. 49), will probably convince the reader

Fig. 49

that bonspiels played out in the open on the old Scotch Lochwinnoch plan may have proved fully as exciting as that indoor match in which a son of Victoria took part, and finally, that curlers, if they so choose, may play with irons and yet be princes of the game.

## Ontario

Curling would have developed in the Province of Ontario at a much earlier period had it not been for the Napoleonic Wars. Britain was compelled for many long years to keep a great part of her manhood under arms, a situation which prevented emigration to America. This is evidenced by the fact that seventeen years after the victory of Waterloo, Ontario found her population increased from 80,000 to 120,000; in even less time, the Canada Land Company—Scottish to the last man—had succeeded in settling in Ontario so many families of their own race that curling, like Jill, came tumbling after.

But in bringing with them their personal belongings they, like the passengers of the *Hector,* had forgotten their curling stanes; and so, as did their *kuting* forefathers, they began to fashion stones for themselves from ice-borne granite fragments which fortunately were to be had in abundance along the rivers. Welcome as this ready supply of material must have been, the stones when put into play were found to be noticeably dull in comparison with the Ailsas which in later days came into general use.

A small minority of those Ontario pioneers, having settled in forest areas where no curling-stone material was to be had, showed a ready ingenuity in making circular curling blocks out of the wood of beech and maple and banding these heavily with iron to furnish the needed weight; and it is recorded that those iron-bound wooden blocks proved in many instances so satisfactory that they continued in use even after the Ailsas and their like were available from home.

Ontario's pioneer curlers had to meet and overcome a continuous succession of problems in order to enjoy a match game with some of their more or less distant neighbours. Their contemporaries in Quebec had the wide St. Lawrence highway on which to travel in winter, but Ontario had little more than rude forest roads. Quebec's proud story of those journeys of four to five hundred miles is at least equalled by the enterprise and fortitude of the Ontario curlers, for whom a match game was a matter of three whole days—one for going, one for playing, and one for returning.

Curling in Ontario came gradually under the control of regularly organized clubs. The first of these was formed at

Kingston in 1820; and following in the wake of Kingston we have Fergus in 1834, Flamboro in 1835, Toronto and Milton in 1837, Galt, Guelph and Scarboro in 1838, Paris in 1843, Elora in 1847, and within the next ten years the Ancaster, Bowmanville, Woodbridge, Hamilton, London and Dundas clubs.

Toronto has always been the centre of curling activities for Ontario. In 1859 the first bonspiel was held on the ice of Toronto Bay; and in 1874 the Ontario Branch of the R.C.C.C. was formed, with headquarters at Toronto. In a history of Ontario curling written for the Jubilee of the R.C.C.C. in 1888, J. S. Russel had this to say:

> When the Ontario Branch of the Royal Caledonian Curling Club was established in 1874, only twenty out of forty-two clubs then in active existence were connected with the parent club. Two reasons sufficiently account for this seeming apathy, the first being that a Canadian Branch of the Royal had been established with its headquarters at Montreal . . . and the distance was too great to admit of regular attendance at the meetings held there of any deputies from the clubs in Ontario; and the second was that the curlers of the Province of Quebec, then as now, used solid iron blocks, weighing from 60 to 80 lb., in the practice of the game, while those of Ontario used the time-honoured granite stones, conforming in weight and size to the rule of the parent club. . . . This difference in the stones used in the game presented an insuperable barrier to curling intercourse between the curlers of the Provinces, and led to the establishment, in 1874, of a branch of the Royal Caledonian Curling Club for the Province of Ontario, with its headquarters in Toronto.
> From this date, and under the auspices of the Ontario Branch, curling has developed marvellously throughout the whole of the Dominion of Canada.

One of the most notable developments has taken place in Northern Ontario, where Haileybury must be given credit for the introduction of curling. In 1907, New Liskeard curlers were guests of the Haileyburians. Shortly afterwards they secured curling accommodation of their own, and since that time a friendly rivalry has existed between the curlers of the two towns. They participated in the bonspiels of the Northern Ontario Curling Association, which included territory from Mattawa to Sault Ste. Marie, and intertown bonspiels were held at Haileybury, where a four-sheet rink had been erected. In 1931 New Liskeard, through the generosity of Mr. Ed. Horne, discoverer of Noranda, secured a very fine steel-frame, six-sheet rink. Thirty-four rinks attended the first New Liskeard bonspiel, and so successful was the event that steps were taken to organize the Temiskaming and Northern Ontario Curling Association. This is a very active association with a yearly membership for bonspiel purposes averaging over eighteen hundred; approximately sixty rinks attend the bonspiel. The crown of Northern Ontario's curling efforts is, of course, the Dominion Curling Championship for 1950.

Curling has indeed come a long way in Ontario during the past seventy-five years. The old-time game out on the ice of Toronto Bay (Fig. 50) has long since given away to the modern game played within the weather-proof walls of brilliantly lighted curling rinks all over the province.

In curling, as in all else, *the old order changeth, yielding place to new.*

Fig. 50

CHAPTER II

# CURLING IN WESTERN CANADA

*When winds frae off the Prairies blaw*
*And bar the doors wi' driven snaw,*
*The Western Curler — so we read —*
*Makes for the Rink wi' gleesome speed.*

## MANITOBA

SCOTLAND HAS THE GREAT HONOUR OF BEING THE LAND OF curling's nativity; but the Prairie Provinces of Western Canada have as great an honour in being the region in which the game's wondrous possibilities have been given fullest scope for development. There the long, cold, dry winters give assurance that plans for special match games or for successive days of bonspiels can safely be made far in advance of the time specified.

Curlers throughout the prairie provinces readily acknowledge the unique advantage which nature has given them; but they attribute their success in bringing the game to its present high standard to other aids as well. It is said that curling west of the Lakes is regarded with a seriousness which the East has yet to acquire. The following report forwarded from the Manitoba Curling Association would seem to bear out this claim:

BRIEF HISTORY OF THE MANITOBA CURLING ASSOCIATION
Now one of Manitoba's most popular sports, the game of curling began in this province in the year 1876. In that year

142

the curlers went to work and secured sufficient subscriptions to make possible the erection of their own rink in Winnipeg and a club was organized with a membership of 70. The rink was completed by the end of November and the first game of curling ever played in Manitoba took place on the 11th of December, 1876. The game lasted two hours and the losers duly fulfilled their agreement to donate a barrel of oatmeal to the hospital.

In 1880 clubs were formed at Emerson and Portage la Prairie and in the following season there was born the "Winnipeg Granite Club". A club was inaugurated at Brandon in 1883 and one at Stonewall in 1884. February 13th, 1884, was a red-letter day in the curling history of Manitoba when a Grand Provincial Bonspiel was opened. Play lasted two days, ending with a sumptuous banquet. Entries came in from Stonewall, Stony Mountain, Portage la Prairie, Emerson, Brandon and Winnipeg. Three years later clubs were formed at Carberry, Clearwater, Morden and a number of other towns. Space forbids the inclusion of many names and incidents which have a prominent place in the archives of Manitoba's history of curling. One of the famous battles which must be mentioned was that which took place on February 1st, 1879, when the players were City Fathers versus Ordinary People. The Common Folk won, so the Aldermen had to pay a forfeit, an oyster dinner.

In December, 1886, a suggestion that a Provincial Curlers' Association be formed was forwarded to and favourably received by the Portage la Prairie Club. On December 6th, 1888, a meeting took place in the rooms of the Granite Club. Delegates were present from the Portage la Prairie, Carberry, Morden, Stonewall, Stony Mountain and the Granite and Thistle Clubs of Winnipeg. After due discussion the decision was made to form the Manitoba Branch of the Royal Caledonian Curling Club. This became in 1908 the Manitoba Curling Association in affiliation with the Royal Caledonian Curling Club of Scotland and eventually the present Manitoba Curling Association.

The *Annual*, the association's official publication, first appeared in 1889, and there has never been a year in which it has not been issued. It contains a list of office bearers, the constitution, general rules, rules of the game, list of past presidents and vice-presidents, list of clubs affiliated, with names of secretaries, list of honorary life members, and diagrams of Points Game—a veritable mine of curling information.

The first annual report mentions fourteen affiliated clubs with
total membership of 694; in the eighth year there were fifty-
five clubs, at the twenty-fifth anniversary 134, and in 1944,
161 clubs with a membership of 5,500.

The bonspiel held in Winnipeg each February lasts about ten
days. It stimulates interest in the game in all clubs, it brings
together in friendly rivalry the best curlers in the world, and
it has done more to improve the standard of curling than any
other agency.

Carried on during bonspiel week under supervision of the
Council are the competitions for ladies. This has been a
feature of the bonspiel since 1914. In 1925 the M.C.A. Ladies'
Association was formed and has grown rapidly; at the 24th
Annual Ladies' Bonspiel (1949) there were 127 rinks entered.
The association has given official recognition also to a Junior
Association, which was formed in 1927 and has grown to
include juniors and high school students. They hold a bonspiel during the latter part of December; in 1947 the high-
school entry was an all-time high of 192 rinks, of which 132
were from outside Greater Winnipeg.

When we consider that Winnipeg has today more curling clubs than Toronto and Montreal combined, we may well
be impressed. It is said to contain over 6,000 curlers, exclusive of ladies and boys. But we need not confine ourselves to
Winnipeg in remarking on the wonderful advance of curling in Manitoba; for while Quebec has over 70 clubs and
Ontario around 175, Manitoba at the close of the 1948-9 season had 257 affiliated clubs. From one of these, the Flin Flon
Curling Club, the secretary, Mr. V. J. Longmore, has kindly
sent me the following information:

This season (1949-50) we are claiming to be the largest individual curling club in the world, with 121 regular men's and
40 ladies' rinks; we have nine sheets of ice. The Ross Lake
Curling Club, a subdivision of the Flin Flon, has 6 sheets,
with 63 men's and 16 ladies' rinks; and our Collegiate Curling
Club (boys and girls) has 65 rinks. There are approximately
250 rinks in the plant departmental bonspiels, with no dupli-
cations; and it is estimated that 2,000 people take part in the
game of curling in Flin Flon.

High School boys sweeping "in", the winning counter, the last rock, a draw shot on the last end, to win the Manitoba High School Bonspiel, Winnipeg 1947. Note: the boys are sweeping on the left of the Stone using the reverse grip.

The year 1948 was the Diamond Jubilee Year of the Manitoba Curling Association. The annual bonspiel entry was not only a record for Manitoba but a world record. There were entered 182 rinks from Greater Winnipeg clubs and 272 rinks from outside points for a total of 454 rinks, against 62 rinks in 1888. There were available in 1948 eighty-nine sheets of ice.

In conclusion it should be remembered that there are scores of clubs not yet affiliated with any official curling organization, so that the number of curlers in Manitoba is considerably greater than the official figures suggest.

## SASKATCHEWAN

The Saskatchewan Curling Association was organized in Regina in 1904, although the game was played in the province as far back as 1880. Prior to 1904 curling in Western Canada was under the jurisdiction of the Manitoba and North West Territories Branch of the R.C.C.C.

Prince Albert, Rosthern and Battleford are the oldest curling centres in Northern Saskatchewan, records indicating that the game was introduced in these locales by the Mounties. In 1890 two Prince Albert rinks competed in the Winnipeg Bonspiel, making the trip by stage to Qu'Appelle, and thence to Winnipeg by rail. Curling in Regina was begun in 1889, and the following year Qu'Appelle and Indian Head formed clubs.

The following sketch of the first rink constructed and long used by curlers of Silton can perhaps furnish us with more genuine curling history than would many long pages of writing. The walls of this primitive rink building were made up of a number of wooden uprights and cross pieces with hay as a substitute for boarding, while a number of poles stretched across the top and covered with a layer of straw composed the roof. Those walls of hay and that roof of straw enclosed two sheets of ice and together gave all the protection needed from the wind-driven snow. This was Silton's first curling rink. It belongs to the past, having been burned down a number of years back, but a more substantial structure of wood stands today upon the same site.

The Silton rink was only one of many such architectural makeshifts in Saskatchewan. It was not uncommon to see the doors of empty box cars, left during the winter on the sidings, set up temporarily as walls for a curling rink which of course had the usual pole and straw roof; and in many localities the rink itself was an out-door affair, with a small shed at one side as a convenient shelter for the discussion of outstanding

Fig. 51

plays and, perhaps, local politics. As for the game itself, I am informed that in extreme cases where up-to-date curling stones were lacking, large jam or other food tins, filled with cement or frozen sand, were used.

Saskatchewan has by now a far greater number of curlers than has any other province. Of the 373 affiliated clubs over 160 have the membership number of 16; and only a small proportion have membership numbers which are not exact multiples of eight, the number needed to make up one rink. If I am right in my surmise, all this is the result of wise planning; a farmer would not care to drive miles to his rink only to find that every place had already been taken, or that too few had assembled to make up even one game. Games, therefore, would in most cases have to be prearranged, with the aid of the party telephones. Most of the rink buildings in rural Saskatchewan are probably, like the one in Silton, two-sheet rinks, which will furnish playing accommodation for curlers from sixteen farmsteads—more or less—which lie nearest together. This at any rate is my attempt to explain those more than one hundred and sixty "sixteens", and the prevalence of these small clubs would indicate the importance of curling to the people of rural Saskatchewan.

The Saskatchewan Curling Association is using the Primary System to determine the championship rink for the province. The first stage is the District Primary competition; the second the Divisional competitions. For the latter the province falls into two divisions, northern and southern, with centres at Saskatoon and Regina respectively. The final playdowns for the two divisional competitions consist of a series of Round Robins. The third stage is known as the Regional Finals, or the British Consols Reginal Finals, and is a best two out of three series. The final games alternate, year by year, between Regina and Saskatoon.

Similarly, the Saskatchewan Curling Association sponsors a Provincial Junior Curling Competition. This is open to male students who are certified by their principals to be registered for a full year's work and making satisfactory progress. Students must be under nineteen years of age. Each school conducts an elimination competition which is followed by district playdowns. The winner of each district playdown is eligible to enter the provincial playoffs. For the semi-finals the province is divided as in the adult competitions, the winner of the northern semi-finals being awarded the Allan Thompson Trophy and the winner of the southern semi-finals the Don Pells Trophy. The Saskatchewan Co-operative Creameries Trophy is the distinction given to the Provincial Junior champions. This rink is eligible to compete in the inter-provincial events for the Sifton Trophy and the Dominion High School Championship.

## ALBERTA

The history of curling in Alberta is interwoven with the early history of the Manitoba Branch of the R.C.C.C. According to the records, the Lethbridge Club was organized in 1887, and in the following year the Calgary and Edmonton clubs were established. MacLeod was organized in 1898, Anthracite and Banff in 1899 and Medicine Hat in 1900.

Much additional history, however, must remain unknown because of an unfortunate fire in the Manitoba Curling Association's office some years ago which destroyed a large part of Alberta's records. From those preserved and published in the fifth annual of the Alberta Branch in 1909 we are given the following significant facts:

This branch was organized in Calgary on the 23rd of January, 1904. At the bonspiel held in Calgary under the auspices of the Calgary C.C., in the winter of 1902-3 on the occasion of a banquet tendered to the visiting curlers from several towns in Alberta, Major (afterwards Colonel) Walker, a veteran soldier who in the early seventies had come to the North West as an officer of the North West Mounted Police, earnestly expressed the desire to see a "Western" Curling Association formed and a withdrawing from the Manitoba Branch. No definite action was taken along these lines at that time. It was, however, just twelve months later and under similar circumstances that the decisive steps were taken. On this occasion at the banquet table, the same Major Walker moved, "That a meeting of curlers representing every Curling Club at this bonspiel be held tomorrow, January 23rd at 2 o'clock p.m., at the curling rink for the purpose of discussing the advisability of forming a branch of the R.C.C.C., separate from the Manitoba Branch."
The meeting was held at the time and place fixed, and about forty curlers from several parts of Alberta and British Columbia were present. Mr. H. S. MacLeod of Calgary was appointed president of the meeting, and Mr. James Smart was

elected secretary. Major Walker was invited by the president to address the meeting. In his remarks—he stated that he had communicated with Mr. J. P. Robertson, Secretary of the Manitoba Branch as to steps to be taken to form a new branch. He (the Major) was very desirous to see a new Western Association formed, and thought the time had arrived. In concluding his remarks he moved, seconded by J. H. Morris of Edmonton, "That this Meeting proceed to the formation of an Association to be called The Alberta Branch of The Royal Caledonian Curling Club of Scotland." The motion carried with enthusiasm.

The first president of the Alberta Branch was James Smart of Calgary, and the secretary-treasurer was J. R. Miquelon, also of Calgary. For some years the annual bonspiel alternated between the cities of Calgary and Edmonton. On 8th February 1917 a meeting of delegates from the curling clubs located north of the town of Red Deer was held in Edmonton and it was decided that an association should be formed to cover that district. As a consequence the Alberta Branch and the Alberta Association hold their annual bonspiels in Calgary and Edmonton respectively.

In Red Deer there are twelve rinks of high-school students playing twice a week, and the Royal Curling Club of Edmonton has begun to organize curling for boys. Edmonton is also the home of the Granite Club and the Avenue Club. The clubs that go to make up the second list for Alberta present a formidable array of names; and the two lists, north and south, give unmistakable evidence that Alberta with her 188 clubs, 82 centred in Calgary and 106 centred in Edmonton, is gaining rapidly on the two greater curling realms of the West, Manitoba and Saskatchewan.

It should be noted here that in 1948 the North West Territories Curling Association centred at Yellowknife became affiliated with the Dominion Curling Association. In 1945 there were only two clubs operating in the North West Territories—the Con and the Negus, both in Yellowknife. This region has now eight men's and three ladies' clubs.

## British Columbia

From the secretary-treasurer of the British Columbia Curling Association I received the following interesting story of the fortunes of the game in that most western of Canada's ten provinces where the winters are, for curlers, in some places disgustingly mild:

The earliest records of curling in British Columbia, as far as the Association can determine, go back only to 1895 when a club consisting of sixteen members was formed at Kaslo. Rocks were procured from Winnipeg, the first game being played on Kaslo Creek; and later in the same year a Points Competition was held at Mirror Lake, two miles south of Kaslo, when Horace Burke took the medal with a score of nineteen points. The Kaslo Club affiliated with the Manitoba Curling Association as the District of Kootenay Curling Association.

In January 1896 the Kaslo Club went to Nelson and played two rinks of Nelson curlers. During that winter, clubs were organized in Sandon and Golden. On 12th February 1898 the Kootenay Curling Association was organized at a meeting in the Allan Hotel, Rossland, with J. B. McArthur of Rossland as president. This meeting was called during the progress of the first bonspiel to be held in British Columbia, with eighteen rinks representing Rossland, Sandon, Kaslo and Revelstoke. At the annual meeting of the Kootenay Curling Association held in Rossland in December 1906, it was decided to change the name of the association to the British Columbia Curling Association and to apply for affiliation with the Royal Caledonian Curling Club of Scotland. The application was approved by that body and membership granted for the season of 1906-7. At this meeting approval was given to reducing the size of rings from 14 feet to 12 feet. Per capita tax was increased from fifteen cents to fifty cents per member.

At the next annual meeting, held in Cranbrook during the bonspiel, the usual headache of poor ice conditions during the games was discussed, and an effort was made to have the event staged annually at Rossland. It was pointed out that Rossland had the finest curling rink west of Winnipeg, that it consistently had good ice owing to its favourable altitude, was easily accessible and centrally located and offered splendid hotel and saloon accommodation as well as other entertainment features. The motion was lost and the association continued to hold its annual bonspiel upon invitation of member clubs.

In these early days of curling in the province, clubs were formed also at Phoenix, Greenwood, Ashcroft, Lardo, Cranbrook and Trail. Penticton affiliated in 1917, and clubs were formed seven years later at Chapman Camp and Kimberley. The Vancouver Club, first formed in 1912, suffered many reverses and for a time was inactive. It was revived in 1931, and affiliated in the following year. Even then its troubles were not at an end, for its plans for a new building were halted by the war, and its makeshift arrangement for the use of ice at the Forum was terminated when the building was taken over by the military in the winter of 1942-3. But plans for a new building were resumed after the war, and the Vancouver Club hopes that before long it will have one of the best curling homes in the Dominion.

There is a modern artificial-ice curling rink in the civic building in Nelson, and another at Trail. Of the Vernon Curling and Athletic Club, the secretary, Mr. A. Browne, writes:

> We built a new five-sheet artificial-ice curling rink in 1947, at a cost of $42,100. We have now started our third curling season in this new rink, with a membership of about 240 curlers. We hold our small bonspiel, drawing rinks from the adjoining cities and towns, between Christmas and New Year, with an attendance of about fifty rinks.
>
> Our Okanagan Valley annual bonspiel is held in the first week in April, using our own rink and also six sheets in the Vernon Civic Arena. We have an attendance of approximately 72 rinks.

Local bonspiels are held also at Cranbrook, Grand Forks, Nelson, and Trail. Concerning curling activity in Kamloops, Mr. W. E. Neill, secretary of the Kamloops Curling Club, writes:

> Kamloops Curling Club was reorganized in March of 1948 and plans were made to erect an artificial-ice curling rink

with four sheets of ice and a modern clubhouse with coffee bar. . . . A very active ladies' section has been organized. The official opening of the new rink took place in December, 1949, when visiting rinks came from Vernon, Salmon Arm and Merritt, the club being host to some 250 curlers and their friends at the social hour.

The British Columbia Curling Association became affiliated in 1936 with the Dominion Association. Its name naturally suggests the province as a whole; but in fact there are two additional curling associations in British Columbia. We note that one of these is composed principally of clubs within the province, but that one or two are just over the Alberta border so that it has been necessary to cross the line for any bonspiel competitions.

These different associations are, however, by no means differing associations. They owe their existence in all likelihood to a desire on the part of their members to find more opportunities for competition with less difficulty in travelling. The first of these smaller associations, some of whose clubs are listed also in the larger B.C.C.A., is the Selkirk Curling Association. Its members apparently obtain additional opportunities in the way of bonspiel competitions, and why should they not? There are no curling laws, written or unwritten, to prevent them. Their 1944 report on the bonspiel held at Cranbrook declared the affair a great success, with thirty-three rinks taking part—but it concludes with words which are becoming more and more familiar to British Columbia's curlers: "unfortunately the ice was wet". The second additional association is the Crows Nest Pass Curling Association. The following account is taken from an annual report of some years ago:

In spite of the fact that the four clubs comprising this association are widely scattered, they report that they have had a very successful season. The annual bonspiel was held at Blairmore from January 30th to February 1st. Fourteen rinks including two from Lethbridge, Alta., competed for

four cups and prizes. The Fernie Curling Club has many new
members to replace the old-timers who have found the game
a little too strenuous when played steadily during the season.

The above account of curling in the province is necessarily brief and incomplete, but it will give some idea of the
interest there is in the game and of the efforts that have been
made to overcome the literally mountainous difficulties with
which curlers have had to contend in arranging to meet.
Needless to say, the most important recent event in the province was the Dominion Curling Bonspiel held at Vancouver
in March, 1950. Every province was represented with the
exception of Newfoundland, which will enter a rink in the
1951 competition for the Macdonald Brier Trophy. Over
three thousand spectators witnessed the opening of the 1950
playoffs.

# CHAPTER III

# CURLING IN THE UNITED STATES

*A border line which no man ever sees*
*Is a' that parts our two beloved countrees;*
*So curlers iverywhaur — being Brithers A' —*
*Think border lines of no account ava.*

THE FIRST RECORD OF CURLING IN THE UNITED STATES HAS TO DO with Detroit, where a group of men formed the Orchard Lake Club[1] and pioneered the game during the winter of 1831-2. For several years thereafter some of those enthusiasts were wont to play with weighted blocks sawed from hickory trees and shaped with axe and chisel to resemble a curling stone, with handles made of the same material. A few of those old blocks — curios, bearing evidence of many a hard fought battle — are still to be seen.

From Dr. Kerr's *History of Curling* we obtain a chronological record of the different curling clubs. According to Dr. Kerr the game reached Milwaukee in 1845; the formation of the Portage Club followed in 1850; the Philadelphia and the New York Thistle and Caledonian Clubs all came into existence in 1855, and the Boston-New England Club in 1856; the Boston City Club, which at first included Scots only, was formed in 1858, the St. Andrew's Club of New York in the same year, the Paterson Club of New Jersey in 1860,

---

[1]Mr. David Foulis is the authority for the precedence of Pontiac, Michigan, as the oldest club in the United States, but gives no exact date.

155

the Yonkers in 1864, the Detroit in 1865, and a club in Buffalo somewhat later. Of these earlier clubs, as far as we know, only one is still active—the New York Caledonian, which recently celebrated its ninetieth anniversary. The Grand National Curling Club of America was instituted 26th June, 1867.

The affiliated clubs of the Grand National are organized in three districts. The New England district centres at The Country Club of Brookline, Massachusetts, and the clubs in this district include the Boston Curling Club, the Nashua Country Club and the Winchester Country Club. The most interesting competition held at The Country Club each year is for the Howard Stockton Cup, first competed for on 3rd February 1917. For many years this competition has been open by invitation to Canadian rinks as well as to the Grand National member clubs.

The northern New York district includes the Utica Curling Club, the Schenectady Curling Club, the Detroit Curling Club and the Saranac Curling Club. At Utica the leading competition is for the Mitchell Medal, which was first competed for in New York, February 4th, 1885. Since 1916 it has been competed for at Utica, regularly. This competition has also in recent years been opened up to Canadian curlers and other clubs in the Midwest.

At Schenectady the matches are played for the Gordon Medal which was first played for in Buffalo on 19th February 1869. This has been held at Schenectady since 1914 and is still limited to the member clubs of the Grand National.

The third district, which comprises the New York Metropolitan area, centres at the St. Andrew's Golf Club at Hastings-on-Hudson, New York. Their ice is shared by the New York Caledonian Curling Club, the Ardsley Curling Club and the Mahopac Curling Club. Also included in this district are the Farmington Curling Club and the Hartford Curling Club, both of Connecticut. The annual competition at St. Andrew's for the Douglas Medal starting in 1935 has now also been opened by invitation to Canadians.

Nearly all the above-mentioned clubs, along with others now functioning, are within easy reach of the international border. The result of so happy a juxtaposition of friendly enemies can readily be guessed by all who have curled. For more than three quarters of a century an almost unbroken series of curling matches has been going on. In the annuals of the Grand National the reader will find that from 1865 to 1950, only rare seasons have been lacking in these happy journeyings of curlers to and fro across the border.

The first international curling match between Canada and the United States was held on Lake Erie at Buffalo in 1865. There were 23 rinks on each side and 23 matches were played. Canada was the winner by 658 points to 478 for the United States. Over fifty players in this match travelled a distance of 850 miles to play one game.

In 1884 the series of international matches for the Gordon International Medal was first played in Montreal. This series had been held on 52 occasions through 1947 with a total of 36 Canadian victories and 16 United States victories. In Canada the matches have been played in Montreal and in recent years the American matches have been held at Utica and The Country Club, Brookline, Massachusetts.

Certain other Canadian competitions are now open to American curlers and are arousing keen interest. The Royal Caledonian Trophy which was put in play first in 1939 reaches its final stage in Montreal with 16 rinks competing, 13 from various centres in Eastern Canada and 3 from the United States. It is keen competition because the 16 competing rinks evolve from local competitions representing well over 600 rinks. In 1947, 1948 and 1949 Americans have reached the finals in this competition but so far have not succeeded in winning the Trophy. The Lord Elgin Trophy played for in Montreal has also been opened to American competitors. Another delightful opportunity for American curlers to visit Canada is offered by the Seigniory Club, Quebec, where every fall the International Friendly Matches are played.

It is easy to foresee the day when many additional curling associations will be functioning in the western border states, and also to foresee that these transborder contests of the West will soon vie with those of the East, all such meets taking place in each country alternately. Thousands of curlers on both sides of the long borderline stretching from the State of Maine to the State of Washington and from Newfoundland to British Columbia will then gather in friendly competition.

Already, the signs of such a wished for consummation can be discerned. Today a number of United States curling clubs whose locations are too far west to make it convenient to join their "brithers" of the East in these international contests, or to become affiliated with the Grand National, have registered with their nearest Canadian association, and by so doing have confessed the need of a like association in their respective states. In evidence of this, an examination of the clubs listed in two Canadian provinces will show the name of a Detroit club on Ontario's list and the names Eveleth, St. Paul, St. Vincent, Virginia and Halloch clubs of Minnesota and the Drayton club of North Dakota on Manitoba's list. As stated in the rhymed lines heading this chapter, apparently the long borderline between the United States and Canada was never intended for curlers save perhaps to lend an additional stimulus to these great international meets. Otherwise, it is "All one body, We".

All this is just as it should be. The Grand National would seem to have a sufficiently fruitful field within which to do its work entirely east of the Alleghanies; and unaffiliated clubs in sufficient numbers exist, and are now increasing, in the districts of Detroit, Chicago, Duluth, Milwaukee, St.

Paul, Seattle and Tacoma to warrant the successful formation of a number of curling associations.

The precedence of Detroit in respect to curling is easy to understand. It was almost certainly due to the arrival of some curling Scots, emigrating directly from their homeland or from Ontario. Detroit, as its name implies, was founded on the straits connecting Erie and Huron, a natural place for early adventurers first to congregate; and, thereafter, a natural place for an attractive game to find a promising habitat. It is easy to see why the game in subsequent years first spread east rather than west seeing that the East had then the greater population and was more advanced socially.

But today the game would seem to have been caught by the cry of "Westward Ho!" In fact, the West has a chain of curling clubs which is fast outnumbering those of the Grand National. The winter season in some of the curling states lacks the long continued frost enjoyed by the curlers directly north of the border. But whatever differences there may be between the Canadian frost belt and its parallel south of the line, these differences are fast being overcome through the building of artificial-ice rinks; and wherever such are established curling seasons can be drawn out from December to the closing days of March.

A recent report by Glenn Harris, editor of *North American Curling News*, gives the following list of clubs, their founding dates, and a comment on the prospects of curling in the United States:—

Appleton, 1939; Ardsley, 1933; Bemidji, 1934; Boston, 1857; Brookline, 1897; Buhl, 1923; Centerville, 1948; Chicago, 1948; Chisholm, 1925; Clintonville, 1948; Detroit, 1885; Drayton, 1893; Duluth, 1891; Farmington, 1906; Fargo, 1938; Galesville, 1904; Gilbert, 1917; Glencoe, 1937; Hallock, 1926; Hibbing, 1913; Highland Park, 1937; La Crosse, 1917; Lake Mahopac, 1924; Lodi, 1873; Madison, 1920; Mapleton, 1905; Mankato, 1903; Medford, 1915; Milwaukee, 1845; New York (Caledonian), 1855; Pardeeville, 1885; Portage, 1850; Portal,

1915; Poynette, 1875; St. Paul, 1912; St. Vincent, 1938; Seattle (two clubs), 1949; Superior, 1893; Tacoma, 1948; Triumph (the southmost curling club in America), 1884; Virginia, 1908; Waupaca, 1879; Wausau, 1925; Wauwatosa, 1921; Winnetka, 1936.

At present the roarin' pastime is part and parcel of the life of every community here listed, and even though the game's indicated footholds appear thinly spread from Seattle, Wash., to the Eastern Seaboard, curling enthusiasm is in no way curtailed by the vastly separating distances involved.

While a majority of the now active clubs own their own properties, many rent or use municipally owned buildings. Some few are organizations without facilities and others curl outdoors. Several have artificial ice with additional clubs planning its acquisition. Outstanding is the recently renovated Duluth Curling Club which has without doubt the finest curling layout in the entire world. A number have buildings at the drawing board stage. The all over picture of the game never looked better. Every club sees its membership growing each year. All plan progressive measures of some sort— bonspiels are swamped with entrants—and the knowledge of the art of the game is wide spread.

All of which gives rise to the prediction that many curlers now alive will live to see the day when thousands of active curling clubs will exist in the United States.

A "Curling House" to accommodate devotees of the ancient Scottish game of broom and stone has been erected on a two-acre plot just south of Dundee Road on the west side of Skokie Highway near Chicago. The double quonset type of building has four rinks of artificial ice and the total cost was $100,000. It was first used in 1948.

Although there have been out-door curling rinks in the Chicago area for the past 10 or 12 years, the "Curling House" is the first of its kind in Illinois. Plans for it originated with curlers from Indian Hill. Also, Glenview, Skokie and Exmoor Country Clubs members felt frustrated because weather conditions, generally speaking, only allowed them to indulge in their favorite sport for about ten days each year. But with artificial ice, a curling season can, if desired, extend from November to April. The building is 200 feet long and 60 feet wide and is so erected that future expansion is possible. The club lounge is separated from the four curling rinks by several large windows and the spectators may watch the games from their easy chairs.

According to one of Chicago's statisticians on curling and curlers to-day, there are 200,000 active curlers in Canada and more than 500 in this Chicago neighbourhood. This "Curling House" is intended to supplement curling in various neighbouring clubs. In fact, a league, with teams from each of these clubs, has already been formed.

All this expansion would seem to lend substance to the prediction in the article by Mr. Harris that in a little over a generation thousands of active curling clubs will be functioning in the United States.

In matters of curling policy, strategy of play, and personal conduct, United States' clubs, younger though they may be, have absolutely nothing to learn from their contemporaries either from Scotland or from Canada. The following excerpt from an article by a New York curler applies to all true lovers of the game in every land where that game is played:

> Curling is a sport which has everything to commend it and is wholly without any of the drawbacks which are too often urged with justice against other outdoor sports. It is free from such vices as gambling, betting, or professionalism; it is health-giving and invigorating, and equally adapted for the old and the young; it is cheap, its implements cost little and it requires no costly grounds or tracks for its full enjoyment; it inspires friendliness, brotherhood and charity among its devotees, and teaches the value of a cool head, a steady hand, a clear eye, and a cautious judgment. It teaches men to accept defeat gracefully and to wear the honours of victory modestly. It is thoroughly democratic in all its tendencies, and on the ice all men are equal except that the best player is the best man.

Should the above fail to convince some hard-boiled Canadian curler that his "brithers owre the border" fully appreciate and understand all that the game involves, then perhaps a few of their curling DONT'S will force him to admit without the slightest reservation that there is nothing about this Auld Scottish Game that his American *confrères* don't know.

DON'T No. 1. Don't advise your skip. He will attend to the skipping, and players should obey no one else.

DON'T No. 2. Don't destroy the morale of any player by unfair criticism when he makes a bad play; he feels worse about it than you do.

DON'T No. 3. When you are lying six and your skip on the last stone of the end raises an opponent's stone in for shot, DON'T LAUGH.

Many others of their DONT'S could be added to the above. The three examples given are sufficient to show their knowledge of the game even though they are younger in experience than we are in Canada.

Our neighbours south of the line, however, are striving to raise their grand total in bonspiel records to a level with their old-time opponents and as long as they keep on so doing, bonspiels, held in alternate years north and south of the border, will continue to grow both in numbers of participating clubs and in intensity of curling zeal. In fact, the long story of these curling invasions—past, present, and to come—across the international line, will in time provide material for a history of a new kind of Border Wars which have proved and will continue to prove a lasting and an inestimable benefit to all North Americans be they curlers or not. On this great truth Canadian curlers might well greet their U.S. brothers in the rhymed lines:

*That BORDER LINE which splits our lands in two*
*Put CURLING on the map for us and you*
*In mighty spiels that now for mony a year*
*Beneath twa flags hae made it crystal clear*
*That curlers iverywhaur are a' one clan—*
*A Britherhood in miniature of MAN.*

# CHAPTER IV

# TRANSATLANTIC CURLING

*Oh whistle an' we'll come owre ma lads,*
*Just whistle an' we'll come owre ma lads,*
*Though fathers an' mithers an' a' should gae mad,*
*Just whistle an' we'll come owre ma lads.*

(With apologies to Burns)

TRANSATLANTIC TOURS HAVE NOW BECOME A PART OF CURLING history. However, the first tour of Scottish curlers to North America in 1902-3 was effected only after prolonged effort on the part of Canadian and American curlers. From both sides of the border invitation after invitation had been wired or mailed to the R.C.C.C. headquarters in Edinburgh, practically begging that a group of their best be sent over. For twenty years this continued while the cautious Scots—although eager to accept—continued to balance carefully a series of pros and cons. Finally, on April 18th, 1902, the following bit of news made its appearance in one of Edinburgh's leading dailies, *The Scotsman*:

> Yesterday afternoon a meeting of representative curlers was held in the Chambers of Mr. Davidson Smith, C.A., Secretary of the Royal Caledonian Curling Club, for the purpose of considering the question of sending a curling team to Canada and the States. This meeting was the final outcome of many previous invitations from overseas curlers. It was held that, owing to the strong national feeling as to the desirability of cementing closer the ties between the Mother Country,

164

Canada, and the United States, the auspicious moment had arrived when such a proposal should be met by sending three rinks at a cost of £700 to play at Montreal, Ottawa, Toronto, Winnipeg, Pittsburgh, and New York.

A special committee under the chairmanship of the Rev. John Kerr was appointed, whose duty it would be to select the curlers and make all the arrangements for their transportation overseas. A great deal of spade work had been necessary to make that meeting the grand success that it was and the man who had done the most of the work was none other than John Kerr. At a subsequent gathering of R.C.C.C. representatives he reported that he had received encouraging messages in support of an overseas tour from His Excellency, the Earl of Minto, Governor-General of Canada as well as from his two illustrious predecessors, the Marquis of Lorne and Lord Aberdeen; that to these he could add such widely known names as Sir Wilfrid Laurier, the Right Honourable Sir Joseph Chamberlain, Lord Strathcona, Lord Elgin, Lord Mount-Stephen, Lord Mansfield, Lord Breadalbane, and Lord Balfour; that every nobleman of any note in the country was heartily in favour of it; and that the transatlantic clubs were resolved to entertain the team hospitably during their stay in Canada and the United States.

Dr. Kerr kept the United States invitation from the Secretary of the Grand National Curling Association of America for a final tidbit. It reads as follows:

Our Executive Committee was duly held in New York and I was instructed to ask the Royal Caledonian Curlers to Gi'e us a ca' next winter. My conscience! What sights you will have seen before reaching New York from Halifax to Winnipeg and thence through the States to the Ocean!

On December 18th, 1902, the first band of Scottish curlers ever to cross the Atlantic (six rinks in the stead of the three as first proposed), sailed from Liverpool on the

R.M.S. *Bavaria*, and landed at Halifax on December 26th. And oh! the reception they received! I was fortunate enough to have some small share in it and afterwards to be in one of the rinks opposing them. After playing a number

ACCEPTANCE.                              INVITATION.

of Nova Scotia rinks in Halifax, the visiting rinks went on to Saint John, N.B., Montreal, Quebec, Ottawa, Toronto, Winnipeg, Minneapolis, St. Paul, Milwaukee, Chicago, Detroit and New York. They were wined and dined to utter repletion by their hosts on both sides of the border; and the respective governments supplied free transportation and luxurious dining-cars. In fact, if they were given an opportunity to spend even a ha' penny, not a reporter aboard their train ever disclosed such an instance. One might say without exaggeration that never before in the history of America had a group of overseas sportsmen left behind them such an atmosphere of International Goodwill. On February 18th,

1903, almost a year after that meeting in the chambers of Mr. Davidson Smith, C.A., they sailed for home, after having travelled 9,918 miles.

SCOTTISH CURLERS' VISIT TO NORTH AMERICA, 1949.

Now between that initial tour and the one which took place in 1948-9 forty-six long years had intervened and during that extensive period the R.C.C.C. in Scotland and its overseas opponents had on five different occasions crossed brooms on alternate sides of the ocean but under constantly changing conditions especially in respect to America. For in the western portions of both Canada and the North Western States, the number of curlers had more than doubled. In the tour of 1948-9 the Scottish invaders found that Winnipeg was no longer the western outpost of Canadian curling. This time they found awaiting them hundreds of new broomsmen in Saskatchewan, Alberta, and British Columbia; and similarly "owre the border" they were confronted with nearly a hundred new and eagerly awaiting clubs belonging to a second United States Curling Association having jurisdiction over North Dakota, Wisconsin, Minnesota and Illinois.

The R.C.C.C., aware of all this, had had to plan on such a scale as would enable its players to meet this greatly increased number of clubs without a like increase in the total time needed for the tour as a whole. It was an exceedingly simple plan and was as effective as it was simple. Instead of sending the usual contingent numbering around twenty-five members, it was decided to send two teams of twenty-five and twenty-six respectively. Each team was to take on its own arranged half of the awaiting clubs and, further, should it eventually develop that the longer journeys by train were threatening to upset the arranged time limit, the teams would, whenever necessary, travel by plane.

A description of games would excite but little interest. But the result of the games, considered as a whole or viewed in contrast to the all-round results of former tours, might

Sir James Denby Roberts, Bart. of Strathallan Castle, Auchter-
barder, Perthshire, Captain of the Scottish Curling Team (left)
chatting with Ford Frick, President of the National League of
Baseball Clubs, who is also an enthusiastic curler and member
of St. Andrew's Golf Club, Mt. Hope, New York. Photograph
taken during the 1949 visit of the Scottish Curlers.

well prove to be a matter of interest to curlers everywhere.

On December 28th 1948, the new Canadian Pacific liner, *Empress of France*, having on board the curlers from Scotland, sailed into Halifax harbour where they were given a true Canadian welcome by the Hon. Colin Campbell of Toronto, acting on behalf of the Dominion Curling Association. Mr. Campbell's mission also included the pleasant task of conducting the visitors across Canada and entertaining them en route.

Sir James Denby Roberts of Strathallan had been asked by the R.C.C.C. to act as the head of the entire contingent with W. C. S. MacGlashen as captain of the rinks making up team No. 1 and John Monteith acting in a like capacity for team No. 2. No time was lost in getting the stones on Halifax ice.

Mr. H. St. C. Silver of Halifax, skipped a rink against the Scots in 1902-3 and won hands down on that occasion, Dr. Kerr afterwards commenting on the superiority of his play: "Of the curlers in Canada perhaps Mr. Silver of Halifax and Mr. Flavelle of Lindsay impressed me most by their magnificent play." In this recent Scottish invasion at Halifax Mr. Silver skipped a rink and almost won again. He is now ninety-one years of age. I met Mr. Silver at the Lord Nelson in Halifax not long ago, and we "talked curling" for the entire evening. I've played against him in days o' lang syne. He is unquestionably the dean not only of translatlantic curling, but also of the curling fraternity of North America.

Both No. 1 and No. 2 teams played at Halifax, Truro and Moncton. Then team No. 2 made a side trip by plane to Charlottetown while team No. 1 was meeting several rinks centred at Saint John. After that, both teams moved up into the St. Lawrence and Great Lakes country, one of the teams playing at Montreal and then at Quebec while the other team was playing rinks at Ottawa and Toronto.

Up to this time the visitors had more than held their

own; but owing, probably, to the constant wear and tear of
playing continuously as well as meeting, perhaps for the first
time, with curlers of somewhat greater skill, plus the strain
of travel, they began to find themselves more often losers
than winners of games. Especially was this the case in Winnipeg and in places further west.

Ardsley defeated the Scottish "Gervain" rink, the only American
rink to win at St. Andrew's. The Ardsley skip, E. W. Fishe, Jr.,
is measuring to determine the winning stone.

However, the Scottish curlers progressed, each team
playing its prearranged games, from city to city, from province to province and from state to state—from Halifax right
around to New York—proving themselves capable of facing
the best America had to offer and, in general, surpassing their
predecessors of 1902-3. The brief invasion of the United
States under the leadership of Sir James himself proved the

skill, courage and fortitude of the Scottish curlers. Three days of curling at The Country Club, Brookline, Massachusetts, the St. Andrew's Golf Club near New York City and at Utica, three banquets and three nights on a sleeper, proved them to be men of iron. On this quick tour 31 matches were played, the Scots being the victors in 21. In fact they

A scene at St. Andrew's during one of the matches between the Scottish Curlers and the Hartford Curling Club. The Scots brought their own push brooms with them.

started piling up a superiority in points until we find them on February 2nd, embarking from St. John's, Newfoundland, terminating a month-long invitation tour of Canada and the United States, after winning sixty percent of the games played. Naturally, they were in a happy state of mind. They were both satisfied and gratified not only on having come out as far ahead, but equally by the magnificent reception that had been everywhere accorded them.

## CANADIAN CURLERS' VISIT TO SCOTLAND—1950

Late in December, 1949, a group of Canadian curlers embarked for Scotland in response to an invitation from the Royal Caledonian Curling Club. This good-will party comprised fifty-one members and was divided into two teams. Team A was captained by the Honourable E. F. Willis of Manitoba and Team B by N. O. Ralston of New Brunswick. The rinks represented as far as possible a cross-section of the best Canadian curlers.

The visiting curlers found certain differences both in the game and in the conditions under which it is played. As a rule the ice in Scotland is not pebbled. There are no hacks as we know them here but simply pieces of steel placed in the ice. The combination play of the "take-out" and "draw" games that has been adopted in so many parts of Canada was not seen to any extent and, indeed, is not popular in Scotland. There, the draw game is the big thing and the players are remarkably skilled in throwing their shots to the indicated position in the ring. Usually the "house" is filled for they seldom try to knock out any of the stones. These differences did not prove too serious a handicap, however, and the Canadians were not long in adjusting their play.

A summary of the results of the tour (combining the records of both teams) shows that out of 76 matches played, the Canadians won 54, tied 1, and lost 21; out of 446 games, the Canadians won 252, tied 27, and lost 167. In view of this very creditable record it is fair to mention that a team of Perth ladies beat the Manitoba rink in a close match, to the delight of the other Canadians and the crowd.

The programme also included a series of test matches for the Strathcona Cup. These matches were played at Glasgow, Perth, Kalkirk, Ayr, and Edinburgh. The results were determined by the combined point total of the two teams, as against the Scottish teams, each team playing five matches.

Although the Canadians won six of these ten matches, the Scots outscored them by a margin of thirty points (Scotland —830; Canada—800), and therefore retained the Strathcona Cup.

The Canadians were tendered the well-known Scottish hospitality at every point en route and returned home full of enthusiasm and truly convinced that we are brithers a'. A group of the Canadian curlers extended their tour by a week's visit to Switzerland as guests of the Swiss Curling Association. There they played on the open-air rinks and it was their unanimous opinion that this was curling under the most perfect conditions. The Swiss curlers play only the draw game and found the Canadian combination style of play difficult to contend with.

The value of these matches in good will and mutual understanding cannot be overestimated and it is hoped that every effort will be made to hold more and more international contests. The glorious game of curling knows no borders.

# PART THREE

# The Modern Game

# CHAPTER I

# SPECIAL SELECTIONS TAKEN FROM THE R. C. C. C. CONSTITUTION

*Each kingdom has its written code,*
*Even the Lilliputian;*
*So curlers, too, have à la mode*
*A written Constitution.*

THE CONSTITUTION OF THE R.C.C.C. FORMS THE BASIS OF THE constitution of every curling club that is affiliated with the mother organization in Scotland; and the most recent R.C.-C.C. *Annual* can always be had on application by the clubs affiliated. This being so it can readily be seen that to have included all its chapters and sections as a part of this book would have served no useful purpose. Yet, there are certain sections, those concerned with "Rules of the Game" and of "Points Competition", along with sundry explanations dealing with rink measurements and accoutrements, which have a more direct appeal to the individual curler and for this reason they have been included here. The order of numeration has not been maintained although reference is made in each case to the section of the Constitution from which the particular excerpt has been taken. Certain slight changes in the wording have been introduced in order to incorporate terms and procedures that have gained general acceptance on this continent.

177

## THE RINK

(From Chapter VI, R.C.C.C. Constitution)

The length of the rink from the foot score (hack line) to the tee shall be 42 yards.

The tees shall be 38 yards apart—and, with the tees as centres, circles having a radius of not less than 6 feet nor more than 7 feet shall be drawn. Additional inner circles may also be drawn.

In alignment with the tees, lines, to be called central lines, may be drawn from the tees to points 4 yards behind each tee, and at these points foot scores 18 inches in length shall be drawn at right angles, on which at 6 inches from the central line, the heel of the crampit shall be placed; when, however, a hack is preferred, it shall be made 3 inches from the central line and not more than 12 inches in length. When hack and crampit are both being used in the same rink, the hack shall be placed immediately in front of the crampit.

Other scores (lines) shall be drawn across the rink at right angles to the central line as in the diagram, viz.:

(a) A hog score (line), distant from each tee one-sixth part of the distance between foot score and the farther tee.

(b) A sweeping score (tee line), across each outer circle and through each tee.

(c) A back score (back line), behind and just touching the outside of each outer circle.

Note: Diagram drawn on the ice shall be referred to throughout the Rules as THE RINK.

## The Rules of the Game

### (From Chapter VI, R.C.C.C. Constitution)

1.  All curling stones shall be of a circular shape. No stone, including handle and bolt, shall be of greater weight than 44 lbs., or of greater circumference than 36 inches, or of less height than one-eighth part of its greatest circumference.

2.  No stone shall be substituted for another (except under Rule 3 or 13) after a match has been begun, but the sole of a stone may be reversed at any time during a match, provided the player be ready to play when his turn comes.

3.  Should a stone be broken, the largest fragment shall be counted for that head (or end)—the player being entitled to use another stone, or another pair during the remainder of the match.

4.  Any stone which rolls over, or comes to rest on its side or top, shall be removed from the ice.

5.  Should the handle quit the stone in delivery, the player must keep hold of it; otherwise he shall not be entitled to replay the shot.

6.  Every stone which does not clear the hog score shall be a hog, and must be removed from the ice, but no stone shall be considered a hog which has struck another stone lying in position. A stone passing the back score, and lying clear of it, must be removed from the ice, as also any stone which in its progress touches the swept snow on either side of the rink.

7.  All matches shall be of a certain number of heads or shots (or ends) or by time as may be agreed on, or as fixed by an umpire at the outset. In the event of competitors being equal, play shall be continued by all the rinks engaged for one or more ends or heads, as may be agreed on, or as may be fixed by the umpire, until the match has been decided.

8.  Every rink of players shall be composed of four-a-side, each player using two stones, and playing each stone alternately with his opponent. No player shall wear boots, tramps, or sandals with spikes or other contrivance which may break or damage the surface of the ice. The rotation of play observed during the first end or head of a match shall not be changed. Any rink not having its full complement of four players shall be disqualified, except in the case of illness or

accident during the match, in which case the lead shall play four stones. If the lead be compelled to retire the second player shall play four stones.

9.    The skips opposing each other shall settle by lot, or in any other way they may agree upon, which party shall lead at the first head or end, after which the winners of the preceding head or end shall lead.

10.    The skip shall have the exclusive regulation and direction of the game for his rink, and may play last stone, or any part in the game he pleases, but he shall not be entitled to change his position when that has been fixed. When his turn to play comes, he shall, if not already arranged, select one of his players to act as skip in his place, and take the position of an ordinary player. He shall not have any choice or direction of the game till he returns to the tee as skip.

11.    Players, during the course of each head or end, shall be arranged along the sides, but well off the centre of the rink, as the skips may direct; and no one, except when sweeping according to rule, shall go upon the centre of the rink, or cross it, on any pretext whatever. Skips only shall be entitled to stand within the circle. The skip of the playing party shall have the choice of place, and shall not be obstructed by the other skip in front of the tee, while behind it the privileges of both, in regard to sweeping, shall be equal. No player other than the skips acting for the time being may stand behind the circle while play is proceeding.

12.    Each player must play from the hack or crampit and must release the handle of the stone before the stone has passed the sweeping score. Left-handed players shall play from the hack or crampit placed on the opposite side of the central line from that used by right-handed players.

13.    Each player must be ready to play when his turn comes, and must not take more than a reasonable time to play. Should a player play a wrong stone, the stone which ought to have been played shall be put in its place.

14.    If a player should play out of his turn, the stone so played may be stopped in its progress and returned to the player. Should the mistake not be discovered until after the stone has come to rest or has struck another stone, the head or end shall be continued as if it had been played properly from the beginning, and the player who missed his turn shall

play the missed stone as the last stone on his side for that end. In the event of two stones being played in succession by one side in error the head or end shall be declared null and void.

15. The sweeping shall be under the direction and control of the skips. The player's party may sweep the ice from the hog score next the player to the sweeping score, and any stone set in motion by a played stone may be swept by the party to which it belongs. Skips only shall be allowed to sweep behind the tee. When snow is falling or drifting, the player's party may sweep the ice from sweeping score to sweeping score. The sweeping shall always be to a side, and no sweepings shall be left in front of a running stone. Both skips have equal right to clean and sweep the ice behind the sweeping score, except while a player is being directed by his skip. At the end of any head or end either of the skips may call upon all players to clean and sweep the entire rink. If objected to, this shall be subject to the approval of the umpire.

16. (a) If, in sweeping or otherwise, the course of a running stone be affected by any of the party to which it belongs, it may, in the option of the opposing skip, be put off the ice; but if by any of the adverse party, it shall be placed where the skip of the party to which it belongs shall direct. Should the position of any stones be altered by such affected stone the skip opposed to the party at fault shall have the sole right to replace them. (b) Should any played stone be displaced before the head or end is reckoned, it shall be placed as nearly before as possible where it lay, to the satisfaction of the skip opposed to the party displacing. If displaced by any other party, both skips should agree upon the position to which it is to be returned; but if they do not agree, the umpire shall decide. (Most Associations here add, "if marred in the course of play after delivery by anything foreign to the game, the player shall re-play the stone.")

17. A rink shall score one shot for every stone which is nearer the tee than any stone of the opposing rink. Every stone which is not clearly outside the outer circle shall be eligible to count. All measurements shall be taken from the tee to the nearest part of the stone. Disputed shots shall be determined by the acting skips; if they disagree, by the umpire; or, when there is no umpire, by a neutral curler chosen by the

skips. No measuring of shots shall be allowed previous to the termination of the head or end.

18. If from any change of weather after a match has begun, or from any other reasonable cause, one party should desire to shorten the rink, or change to another, and if the two skips cannot agree, the umpire shall, after seeing one head or end played, determine whether and how much the rink shall be shortened, or whether it shall be changed, and his decision shall be final. In no case, however, shall the rink be shortened to less than 32 yards from the foot score to the tee. Should there be no umpire, or should he be otherwise engaged, the two skips may call in any neutral to decide, and his powers shall be equal with those of an umpire. The umpire shall, in the event of the ice appearing to him to be dangerous, stop the match. He shall postpone it, even if begun, when the state of the ice is in his opinion not fitted for testing the curling skill of the players. Except in very special circumstances, of which the umpire shall be judge, a match shall not proceed, or be continued, when a thaw has fairly set in, or when snow is falling and likely to continue during the match, nor shall it be continued if darkness comes on to prevent the played stones being well seen by players at the other end of the rink. In every case of such postponement to another day the match when renewed, must be begun *de novo*.

### SETTLEMENT OF DISPUTES

(From Chapter XI, R.C.C.C. Constitution)

(a) Should any dispute arise between clubs or players owing to the umpire's decision, it shall be referred to an arbiter to be appointed, failing agreement, by the council.

(b) The arbiter's award shall, except with respect to the umpire's right of appeal to the council, be final and binding on both parties.

(c) The council shall only have power to overturn the same if the procedure has been irregular. Their decision shall be final.

(d) Any complaint as to irregularity must be lodged with the Secretary of the Royal Club within ten days of the date of the award.

(e) Should the procedure be found irregular, the council shall set aside the award, and order the disputants to begin the reference anew.

## Rules for Local Competitions

### (From Chapter XII, R.C.C.C. Constitution)

#### POINTS GAME

(a) Competitors shall draw lots for the rotation of play, and shall use two stones.

(b) The measurement of the rink for points play shall be in conformity with the provisions of Chapter VI (Constitution).

(c) Two circles, one having a radius of 4 feet and the other having a radius of not less than 6 feet and not more than 7 feet, shall be drawn round each tee, and a line through the centre of each circle from the foot score to the hog score.

(d) Every competitor shall play four shots at each of the nine following points of the game, viz: (1) Striking, (2) Inwicking, (3) Drawing, (4) Guarding, (5) Chap and Lie, (6) Wick and Curl in, (7) Raising, (8) Chipping the Winner, and (9) Drawing through a Port according to the definitions and diagrams here given.

(e) In Nos. (2), (6), (8) and (9), and at (10) outwicking, when played, the object stones shall be placed so that two shots shall be played on the right at one head or end and two on the left at the other head or end.

(f) No stone shall be considered outside a circle unless it be entirely clear of that circle.

(g) In the event of two or more competitors being equal, they shall play four shots at (10) Outwicking. If the competition be still undecided, the umpire shall order that one or more of the preceding points be played again by the competitors who are equal.

Note 1.—No scores made in local competitions shall be reported in the *Annual* unless these have been conducted under the above rules.

Note 2.—Much time will be saved if two rinks be prepared lying parallel to each other, the tee of the one being at the reverse end of the other rink; every competitor plays both stones up one rink and afterwards both down the other, thus finishing at each round all his chances at that point.

Diagram To Be Drawn On the Ice Before Playing

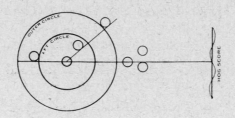

### 1. Striking.

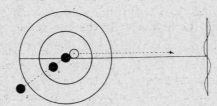

A stone being placed on the tee, if struck, shall count 1; if struck out of the outer circle, it shall count 2.

### 2. Inwicking.

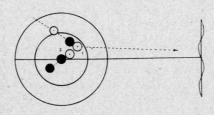

A stone being placed on the tee, and another with its inner edge 2 feet 6 inches from the tee, and its fore edge on a line drawn from the tee at an angle of 45° with the central line; if the played stone strike the latter on the inside, it shall count 1; if it perceptibly move both stones, it shall count 2.

### 3. Drawing.

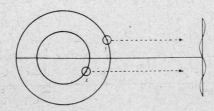

A stone being played, if the same lie within or on the outer circle, it shall count 1; if within or on the 4 foot circle it shall count 2.

### 4. Guarding.

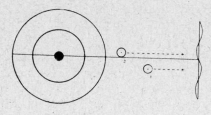

A stone being placed on the tee, if the stone played rest within 6 inches of the central line, it shall count 1; if on the line it shall count 2. It must be over the hog, but must not touch the stone to be guarded.

### 5. Chap and Lie.

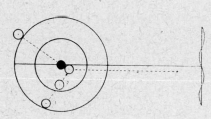

A stone being placed on the tee, if struck out of the outer circle, and the played stone lie within or on the same circle it shall count 1; if struck out of the outer circle, and the played stone lie within or on the 4-foot circle, it shall count 2.

### 6. Wick and Curl in.

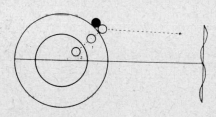

A stone being placed with its inner edge touching the outer circle, and its fore edge on a line making an angle of 45° with the central line, if the same be struck, and the played stone curl on or within the outer circle, it shall count 1; if struck, and the played stone curl on or within the 4-foot circle, it shall count 2.

### 7. Raising.

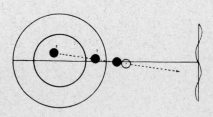

A stone being placed with its centre on the central line and its inner edge 8 feet in front of the tee, if it be struck into or on the outer circle, it shall count 1; if struck into or on the 4-foot circle, it shall count 2.

8. Chipping the Winner.

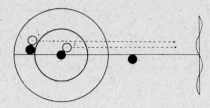

A stone being placed on the tee, and another with its inner edge 10 feet in front, just touching the central line, and half guarding the one on the tee, and a third stone being placed 4 feet behind the tee, with its inner edge touching the central line, but on the opposite side from that on which the guard is placed, if the played stone strike the stone placed behind the tee, it shall count 1; if it strike the stone on the tee, it shall count 2.

9. Drawing through a Port.

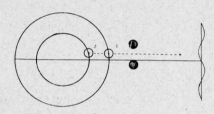

A stone being placed with its inner edge on the central line 10 feet in front of the tee, and another stone on the opposite side and with its inner edge 2 feet from the central line, if the played stone pass between these two stones without touching either, and rest within or on the outer circle, it shall count 1; if within or on the 4-foot circle, it shall count 2.

10. Outwicking.

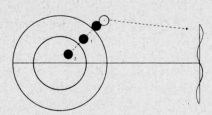

A stone being placed with its inner edge touching the outer circle and its centre on a line making an angle of 45° with the central line, if struck within or on the outer circle, it shall count 1; if struck within or on the 4-foot circle, it shall count 2.

## The Umpire

(From Chapter XIII, R.C.C.C. Constitution)

1. The duties and powers of an umpire shall be the general superintendence of a match or competition, the power of settling disputed shots, and other questions that may arise in course of play.

2. He shall, at the request of the secretary of either Club, fix the day, the hour, and the ice most suitable and mutually convenient, giving at least twenty-four hours' notice to the secretaries of both Clubs.

3. He shall satisfy himself that all the players are duly qualified, or have been previously agreed to.

4. He shall fix the terms of the match (whether by time, shots or ends), if not mutually agreed upon by the competing Clubs.

5. He may depute a neutral curler associated with the Royal Club and acquainted with the Rules to act in his stead; but the report of the match shall be countersigned by him.

6. In the event of the match being played on the ice of either parties (when the visitors may select the rinks), he may be called upon to approve of the ice and rinks upon which the match is to be played.

7. He shall have power to decide whether it be necessary to shorten or change the rinks, should the skips not agree, or to postpone the match, even if begun, when in his opinion the state of the ice, or the weather, is not such as to test the curling skill of the players.

8. He shall, in the event of the competitors being equal, direct that play be continued by all the rinks engaged for one or more heads or ends, as may be necessary to decide the match, or that one or more Points be played again by the competitors who are equal in the Points Game.

9. He shall, in all cases, call for objections from the losing Club before awarding the medal, and thereafter forward a Report of the Match to the Secretary of the Royal Club, giving the information required on the form provided for that purpose.

10. He shall have the power to award the medal off-hand to the Club which appears on the ice, should the other Club be absent without a reason satisfactory to him.

11. His decision in respect of all questions affecting the match shall be final, unless appealed against.

12. He may appeal to the council against the award of the arbiter.

## INITIATION

### (From Chapter XIV, R.C.C.C. Constitution)

1. Any two initiated members of the Royal Club may initiate the members of a Local Club.

2. Certificates of Initiation, signed by the secretary of the Royal Club, may be issued to initiated members of Local Clubs by their secretaries who shall countersign and date them.

## ALTERATION OF RULES

### (From Chapter XV, R.C.C.C. Constitution)

1. No new rule, alteration, or repeal of an existing rule shall be made unless at the annual meeting or at a meeting specially called for the purpose, and unless approved by two-thirds of the representatives present and entitled to vote. Notice of any proposed alteration shall be given.

A brief explanation of why the lines and circles used in marking out a rink were brought into being, followed by a few comments on the questionable value of Points Playing as a genuine test of curling ability, may not prove altogether amiss.

The lines and circles marking out a rink and reported as having come into existence one by one, were due to invention's greatest master, Necessity. At first the tee is said to have been free of circles seeing that in the old coiting days it was looked upon rather as a mark to be aimed at than, as it was later to become, the centre of skipping strategy for the winning of ends. Viewing it in another way the tee in ancient days was an end in itself.

This central spot has had at different times and places a variety of names; it was not only known as the tee but also as the *toesee*, the *cock*, "Wha will they station at the 'cock' ",— the *cockee*, the *wittyr* or *witter*, the *gog* and *gogsee*. But all these names have mostly been laid aside save the now familiar term "tee". Curlers since almost from the beginning of the last century have had no need actually to see the tee when delivering the stone. Our Scottish brethren not so far back were wont to make use of a coin or button to mark the tee as indeed we ourselves here and there may be still in the habit of doing. These minute bits of markings, however, were, in the Old Land, somewhat improved upon by using a larger mark consisting of a circular piece of iron having a sharpened prong underneath, which was pressed hard down into the ice. But perhaps if not the oldest then the oddest of those old-time tee markers was a wooden pin standing a foot high so as to be clearly seen from the opposite end of the rink. It may just possibly have been that those Kilquhar men of pith used such bottle-shaped pieces of wood when they played those lantern-illuminated all night games which ceased only at the sunrise crowing of the cock. Yet laugh at those clumsy looking affairs as you will, they are said to have remained so popular that no longer than fifty years ago they were reported as being used by the Alloa Club.

The first circles are said to have varied in diameter from 2 to 12 feet. The spaces enclosed were known as "broughs" while practically the whole area around the rings was styled the "boardhead". The reason for the first drawing of a circle around the tee was due to no chance incident. Circles were a crying need for the determining of the exact distances of disputed shots from the tee. Think of the many old-time squabbles they must have silenced!

The hog line, as every curler knows, was an additional godsend to the game. In its place, 7 yards from the tee and crossing the central line at right angles, it becomes a curling Rubicon. The stone failing to cross this line, except in case it was blocked by another stone also on the hog score, is at once removed as serving no further purpose except to obstruct the game. That somewhat fanciful waving line drawn crossing and recrossing the hog score serves no purpose with us in Canada, but in Scotland it serves a very useful purpose. Curling in the Old Land is still frequently played on  lochs, tarns and ponds, on each of which are seen at times a number of cracks in the ice and often one of these cracks happening to run close alongside and parallel to the hog line would be in danger of being taken for the same. Hence this waving line serves to mark the true line from the counterfeit.

From the hack to the farther tee is 42 yards; and from the same hack to its own tee is 4 yards, making in all the standardized rink of 46 yards. And here we are faced with this question—why was 46 yards instead of old Tam Haddow's 49 yards or the old-time 30 yards, agreed upon as the all-time future length for a curling rink? To answer this question one has only to think back: when the heavy-weight stones were tabooed the 30-yard rinks were no longer necessary. In fine, it was the tabooing of the heavy multiform stones and the incoming of the lighter circular stones that gave the player of average strength the long delayed opportunity to show what he could do. At last he could select his very own pair of stones wholly with the idea of having them of just such weight as would never cause him in the critical moment of delivery to worry as to how much strength to use. With stones he can easily handle he learns through continuous and patient practice to carry on with the growing sense of mastery,which comes with success.

What has all this to do with the wisdom manifested in

standardizing a rink's length at 46 yards? It has just this to do with it: the curler to succeed must, at delivery, give the strength needed—no more—no less. With men of average strength—each using a stone he can easily handle—it has been found, after the player has made his delivery in the direction and with the turn asked for, that the stone will begin to curve just as it enters the ring area. And to do all this the player should have 42 yards of running space—not 49 or 30 but 42 and add to this 42 the remaining 4 yards to hack No. 2 and we have our 46 yards.

Concerning the central line which runs from hack to hack I have only this to say, that it is a line which beginners from their first day on the ice must learn to avoid as a guidance to the hand when delivering the stone. They must learn to keep their eyes on the upright broom of the skip and the hand will in time begin automatically to deliver the stone in line with the direction marked out by the eye. In fact, it was this very point I had in mind when composing the second verse of the poem *The Spirit O' Curling*:

> She kens ilka laddie o' curling maun learn
> How to play on the broom wi' the hand and the ee;
> How to lay doun a guard wi' an oot—or inturn;
> How to wick and curl in on the face o' the tee.

As far as I have been able to observe, Points Curling, valuable as it is from the standpoint of practice, seldom inspires the curlers—in the words of Burns—"to flock thitherward wi' gleesome speed". Furthermore, authentic records on points games tend to show that it is not a true test of the curler's skill. This truth in fact, was rather painfully brought home to its founders, the members of the old-time Duddingston Club, when on the second occasion of its being held the gold medal was won by their worst player.

It is a kind of contest wherein, like Scott's celebrated Smith of Perth, each plays for his own hand—but under conditions that few there will feel more out of place than the skips, and for reasons plainly obvious. The chief of these reasons is that the skip is looked up to as the one who should win. One needs—on finding himself thus silently appraised—the coolest nerves to play  as he would if skipping in the ring. But with the leads and second stone men the position is the exact reverse. To state it in a paradoxical way, they in losing have nothing to lose. Even the field of play with only a stone or two in view is a field to which they are more accustomed than are the skips. They may be said to feel there as Rob Roy felt when addressed too familiarly by that name, angrily shooting back the words, "My foot is on my native heath and my name is MacGregor". So may these leads and seconds feel when playing Points that they're real Mac-Gregors on their native heath.

We all have our little prides and prejudices about exhib-iting ourselves — especially when looked upon to excel in trials of skill—and so it may well be with a more or less nervous skip when playing points. Finally to put the whole of the above argument into a rhymed text I might say:

> In playing points—a kind of curlers' solitaire—
> Contesting skips—at times meet fearful Waterloos
> When raw unpractised leads give them with ease the air,
> Then swagger off—heads high—like crested cockatoos.

# CHAPTER II

# TO THE NEW CURLER

## By H. E. Weyman

"One must learn to walk, before one can run" is just as true in curling as it is in life in general, and the new curler must obtain some knowledge and understanding of the "mechanics" used in the delivery of the stone. This requires practice.

There are 10 basic shots which a curler should be master of, namely:

1. The Draw
2. Striking
3. The Inwick
4. The Outwick
5. The Raise

6. The Guard
7. Wick and Curl In
8. Chap and Lie
9. Chap and Roll
10. Chip the Winner

The "draw" is a key shot from which several others originate, such as the "guard", the "raise", etc.: and all curlers, no matter what positions they are playing, will be called upon to play this shot. It is, therefore, essential that the new curler must first learn to draw accurately. While the easiest shot in curling is a draw down either side of the ice sheet to the centre, which any player should be able to do, yet it needs both ability and skill to draw accurately, place guards to dimes and hairlines and to draw across the ice sheet, from the in-turn side to the out-turn side or right of the centre line, and vice versa.

It is customary for the new curler to take the lead's or first man's position on a rink, not because it is the least important position, for it is not, but as most of the shots are "draws", it provides him with an opportunity to develop this basic shot, and at the same time to learn the game. It should be realized that "top notch" curlers are the product of a gradual development, which can be hastened by study and practice. Playing at least two years in each position is time well spent; in fact, there is no better way of getting "nowhere" than by jumping from lead to third or second to skip. Don't stunt your growth as a curler.

It is perhaps appropriate to give a brief description of the rink: It is a mistake to assume from what has been written, that curling cannot be indulged in with considerable enjoyment by poor or indifferent curlers, in fact, by anyone. In no other game is there so much fun, excitement and friendly intercourse as among the less serious, if indifferent curlers, and it is for this reason that curling stands out so singularly in fraternal friendship, unity, and mutual understanding. This fellowship is undoubtedly derived from the fact that the game is played with teams (rinks) of 4 players. Each player has a distinct position on the team, namely, lead (first man), second, third, and skip, or captain, and the play in each position differs in respect to the types of shots.

The Lead: As he is the first man, and there are no stones in the rings, or only one, if the opponent plays first, the predominant shot is the "draw". This may be to the centre or the sides of the rings or in front, and the stones must be fairly accurate in length. If the opponent plays first, then the lead may be required to draw up close to the opponent's rock, or to draw in behind or take it out. This calls for skill and ability.

It is obvious that, should the lead miss his draws or

shots, his rink will be at a grave disadvantage, and might even lose a game, if the playing ability of the two rinks were evenly matched. The play of the leads will often decide the winner. It is surprising how many curlers hold the wrong impression that the lead position is of minor importance.

The Second: In this position the player has more variety of shots, but must be accurate in the draw, for he has to place guards, draw to shots, and raise shots in. In addition, he should be capable of taking shots out, and playing draw wicks if called upon. Experience in the lead position is necessary to meet the playing requirements of this position satisfactorily.

The Third: This position requires an experienced player capable of executing almost any shot, for he is often relied upon to correct or offset mistakes and poor shots of the lead or second. He must be able to draw or guard to a dime, throw deadly runners, chap and roll, etc. A knowledge of skipping and strategy of the game, and experience in judging the ice, is a necessity and an advantage to the skip, who is then able to consult with him when occasion demands. He must have the ability to judge speed and direction and sweeping requirements.

It should be mentioned that in modern curling, the third is a consultant and assistant to the skip, and although he takes charge of the rink while the skip plays his rocks, the final decision as to what shots are to be played, is left to the skip. This is as it should be, for it is the skip who bears the responsibility for the plan and strategy of the play and he may often have to play the vital winning shot.

The Skip: The skip is, of course, the "King Pin" around which the rink and the game revolves. It is he who plans the strategy and directs the players and the game. He holds the position by his ability, experience, and with the consent of his players. It is not always the best curlers who make the best skips. This may seem paradoxical, but is, nevertheless, a fact. Curlers as thirds, seconds, or leads who can execute any shot in the books, draw to a dime, throw deadly runners, raise, chap, wick and guard with a perfection that thrills one to the bone, may be lacking in judgment, be weak in strategy, or generalship, in ability to analyze ice conditions, in self-confidence to make the last shot. A skip should show:

1. *Self-confidence:* Not conceit but confidence that he can make that last shot through his ability of concentrating on the simple mechanics of delivering the stone instead of thinking of the disastrous consequences of missing.

2. *Ability to judge the ice:* This takes practice and experience. On a perfect sheet of ice, it is a comparatively simple matter; but on an uneven surface with "runs" and "fall backs", the calculations of ice are of vital importance. The ability to judge ice also implies a knowledge of weight required. The skip must know what weight his players will use in delivering the rock, then give them the ice corresponding to that weight. The skip must know his players, and they too must know what he expects.

3. *Ability to judge the capabilities of his players:* If the skip has a lead that cannot throw a fast rock, he must give the ice accordingly. If the third is surer at hitting with a fast rock, give the ice required. If the second can draw better than hit, give him draw shots, when possible. If a player is surer with an in-turn, give him that turn, when possible. The skip must study the weak and strong points of each player. Always get the most out of every shot.

4. *Ability to fit in with his players:* Even in modern curling, far too many skips crab at their players when they miss. Nothing upsets the curling ability of the rink more than this. Remember, the player feels badly enough when he misses. Don't make it worse, or he will lose his confidence, and the infection will spread to others. A good skip will always be cheerful and will commend good shots. He will keep quiet, or sympathize with a player who has made a poor shot. If he can keep up the spirits of his rink, whether winning or losing, the players will play better.

5. *Optimism:* The never-give-up spirit is important in any game, and it is even more important in curling. Stick to

it even if you are down 10 points, for you'll never win a game if you give up hope.

6. *Ability to pick a well-balanced rink:* Four skips, or three or even two will never make a good rink. A good skip will have the ability to select players, who have potentialities and who fit in with each other and play well together. They must have sufficient confidence in his ability as skip, and be willing to play the shots he gives without question. A good skip will take the players into his confidence, and will discuss important decisions with them, so as to develop the feeling of "all for one and one for all".

A word of WARNING to the rink: Never forget that when a member of a rink begins to feel that he can skip better, knows more and plays better than the skip, he should immediately get off that rink, for he is of use neither to the rink nor to himself.

## The Game

Literally speaking, it can be said that there are three different types of games in curling, namely:

1. The Dead Draw Game;

2. The Heavy Draw or Aggressive Game;

3. The Knock-out or Take-out Game.

*The Dead Draw Game* is the old original type, wherein the height of curling was reached, when most or all the stones remained in the rings at the completion of an "end". It is essentially a slow game where the wicks, raises, and many other shots are made with draw weight. It was permissible gently to move shots to the back, but it was distinctly ungentlemanly to be fast enough to knock opponents' rocks out of the ring, or to break up bunches or clusters of them. In this type of game, all play is subordinate to and culminates in the play of the skip, who is the only predominant player.

The lead and second players are confined to draw shots, while the third has more of a variety according to circumstances. As may be expected with a draw game of this nature, there are always quite a number of stones in or near the rings, which present opportunities for wicks, raises, rubs, etc. The possibilities for lucky shots and flukes are considerably more in this style of game than the other types of games, and accuracy is not of such paramount importance. It is a quiet game, somewhat dull, with little action or excitement.

Although this type of game has been superseded by more modern ones, it is still played in a few places, more particularly in the Province of Quebec, where it is played with 60-pound irons, instead of the granite rock. The purpose of the weight is to "anchor" the shots, making them harder to move once they reach their position. Draws, wicks, rub-ins, etc., are easily made, which would not be possible with the granite rock owing to its liveliness. Should the player have more weight than intended, no damage of consequence would result, whereas with the granite considerable damage would occur.

*The Heavy Draw or Aggressive Game* is really a modern development of the old Dead Draw Game. In fact, it is known in many quarters as the Draw Game. The game is a combination of the Dead Draw and Take-out games, where heavier draw weight is used for wicks, take-out shots, etc., sufficient just to pass them through the rings. It can be described as a more open democratic game, where each player has a variety of shots, demanding greater accuracy and a more equal distribution of responsibility for ultimate success. As a general rule there are not a great many stones in or around the rings at any one time, and the opportunities for wicks, raises, etc., are not as numerous as with the Dead Draw Game. There is less possibility for lucky shots and flukes. This type of game has life, action and excitement, which have made it popular and attractive to young and old alike.

*The Take-out or Knock-out Game* is the most difficult of all types of games to play, and requires the most skill. Each player from lead to skip may be called upon to make any shot in the books, draw to a hair, throw runners, raise, or chip, etc., the last rock often being the vital one. It is definitely the wide open game in curling, where heat and pressure on the nervous system is at the maximum. Dead ends (no score) are not uncommon, while with well-balanced rinks, the scoring is generally one or two points at a time. It is seldom that more than a few rocks are in or around the rings. There is little opportunity for wicks, raises, etc., but when present and played, they are spectacular. With a wide open game of this description success depends on the ability of each player making his shot. A "miss" by one, be it the lead or the skip, the second or the third, can seldom be recovered. In contrast with the other types of games, particularly the Dead Draw, each player's curling ability is clearly defined. He may be required to take out a shot with a fast runner, and draw to a dime with his next rock, or to draw to or take out shots on the sides of the rings, requiring considerable skill, for they may be the only shots in the rings. A "miss" may give an opponent a tremendous advantage. The strategy plays are important, as are the position of the rocks. The last stone on the last end imposes considerable pressure on the skip.

This style of game is full of action and excitement, for changes in the fortunes of war are rapid and there is always a pronounced element of danger that the shots may be missed. While the skip must often make the last rock count, he is not the autocrat, or the only spectacular curler on the rink. It is essentially "all for one and one for all".

*Versatility*: Each type of game has its adherents, but modern curling has developed the versatile rink, which through time and practice, is just as proficient in one type as in the other. Most of the better class rinks are sufficiently versatile as to be able to switch from one style to the other, whenever they wish. Such rinks possess considerable advantage over those which are proficient in one style only. It is generally admitted that proficient rinks at the Draw Game cannot compete with equally proficient rinks at the Aggressive Draw or Take-out Games. Neither can any of them compete with the versatile rink. The basic shot is the draw, at which both the Aggressive and Take-out enthusiasts must, of necessity, be proficient as well as at the faster shots, for one of the most difficult plays in curling is a fast shot and then a draw to the button. Those who restrict themselves to the Draw Game have neither the sense of feel, nor the technique for the faster shots. One of the main reasons that the western curlers are practically unbeatable today is that they have fully developed the versatile rink.

*Strategy*: The plan or strategy of the game and play-making possibilities, devolves on the skip, and necessitates considerable study and experience. It is for this reason that rinks with older men as skips and thirds are more successful. In the heat and excitement of a tight game, the seasoned and mature curler with experience is necessary to hold the game and the players within control. It is the skip who plans the strategy, directs the game, and decides the shots for the players. While many of his decisions cannot obviously be conceived beforehand and must be made to meet conditions as they arrive, yet there are certain basic principles of play and strategy, with which the members of any rink which intends to develop, should be familiar. Not only should the players have some knowledge and understanding of the general strategy, but that knowledge will be beneficial to the skip himself. It is well to remember that the points enumerated herewith may not always meet prevailing conditions:

1. Remember, that during the first two or three ends until the pebble has worn off the surface, less ice is required. As the game proceeds, the amount of ice required will increase. For example, only 6 inches may be necessary on the first end. This might increase to 2 feet later on.

2. For the first few ends, "Take-out" shots should be played firmly. It may take a lot of weight to reach the rings until the pebble is worn down.

3. It is good practice for the skip to give the lead an in-turn and an out-turn the first two ends. This will give all players a general idea how the turn works on that particular ice sheet. Each player should watch such shots.

4. Remember, stones on the side of the house are harder to hit than those in the centre of the rings.

5. Knowledge of the characteristics of the ice and its runs and fall-backs may easily decide the game. A good rink will pay close attention to the "run" of the rocks and the players gain a better understanding of the ice itself and just why the skip is giving the shot and the ice. A curler must learn to "read the ice".

6. Remember, the outside ice is always slower than that in the centre of the sheet. Allow for it.

7. Play for a roll when taking out an opponent's rock. Try to strike it so that your rock rolls to a different place in the rings or behind a guard.

8. If your opponents' rocks are lying in the front part of the rings, be sure you hit them, don't guard. If they lie behind the tee, draw to them, for they will give you a good backing, making it hard for your opponent to get your stone.

9. Don't play too fast when moving a single shot from the rings. Your stone is no good at the back of the house, if you miss. On the other hand, it may be fatal to be short.

10. It is often better to be longer than to be short. Don't guard an opponent's rock.

## The Skip and Playmaking

Rules of etiquette and sportsmanship indicate that the skip giving directions and the broom, be entirely free of interference of any nature. The opposing skip is expected to stand back free of the rings, in order to give full freedom to the skip who is directing his player. After the rock has been delivered both skips have equal right in the rings, but it is not good etiquette for the opposing skip to sweep a rock before it has crossed the tee line.

Rules for the Skip:

1. Know how to play your men and know in what positions they are best.

2. Watch for the weakness in your opponents. If they are poor in hitting, make them hit. If they are poor at the draw, play plenty of guards.

3. Should your player be better on the draw, and you are down one or more, give him a full draw to the front of the opponent's shot to get a backing, which will require your opponent to play a fast shot to get rid of yours. If you are several points up, it would be better to have your player play a shade over draw weight and just touch your opponent's back. On the other hand if your player is better at hitting than drawing, it would be better to have him take the shot out and try for a roll to the outer edges or behind other stones.

4. When playing a game, grab a big end before the others get the feel of the ice. This requires steady draws, but heavy enough to get in the rings. Remember the ice is generally heavy at the start.

5. Figure out your opponents' style as soon as possible; find their weaknesses and how they react to your guards, draws, and take-outs. The character of the individual shots are decided by:

    (a) The qualifications of your players and the opposing players;

(b) The standing of the score;

(c) The style of game adopted.

Remember, every shot should be given with the thought in mind, "What will be my opponent do next, and what kind of a shot will I be forced to give next?"

6. The run of the ice will determine what style of game can be played. Don't try the take-out game if the ice is not suitable.

7. Endeavour to foresee your opponent's strategy and out-guess his intentions. Place your rocks to induce him to set up shots and combinations favourable to you.

8. With an open house, a draw to the outside rings is always good, but should it be the last end, and you have the last rock, sometimes one on the button, setting up the play for a straight exchange of stones so as to count with your last, is good if the score is tied. However, when taking out shots, don't play too fast, or you may lose your touch for draw shots.

9. When you have the last stone, try and keep the front of the house open and free from being cluttered up with rocks. Endeavour to place your rocks all over the rings, starting with the two outside edges. Then put one at the back in the centre. If these are still good, you can then put some in the front or more on the sides.

10. A good skip will not bunch his stones in the rings; he will spread them around so that they will be harder to hit.

11. If the opponent has two stones in the rings, play for the front one. You may get them both. However, this does not necessarily apply in the case of the last rock.

12. Some skips do not like your rocks in front of the house and refuse to play their men close to them for fear of raising them in. In such an event, should they be shot, it is all open for you to take the shot out.

13. Other rinks like the hitting game, in which case you would keep plugging up the front with draw shots, hoping for a miss on their part.

14. Many skips possess only one idea, that is, to be shot after each of the players has played. This is often a mistake.

It would be better to forget that shot for the moment and get another in for second shot, or even place one for a raise or to wick-off later. Then should your player miss taking the opponent's rock out, you will still lie second.

15. Should you be up against a rink very good on the draw game, and unless your own draw game is as good, try and get them shooting at your shots. This will require you to get a shot in a tough place.

16. Should you be up against a stronger rink than your own, you can then only play your strongest style of game, and try to worry them.

17. When a few points up, and there are only a few more stones to be played and a few ends to go, it is often good policy to play all the opponents' rocks out of the rings and hold them down to one point. Don't leave the opponents' rocks in front of the house, for they make good raises or guards to draw around.

18. When you are down in the score, draw to their shots and use them as a backing for yours, but don't set up a cluster of rocks for your opponent to hit or a pocket for him to draw into.

19. When the game is close, try and leave as many stones in front of the rings as possible, and prevent your opponent from getting his rocks into the house. Should they not make their draw shots, you will have your own rocks for raises.

20. On the tenth end in a twelve-end game, it is always well to remember that the last rock on the last end may win the game, and that the winner of the tenth end will likely have that last rock on the last end.

21. When you are shot rock, and your opponent is second close by, play your first stone either to take out his other stones or get yours in for third count, leaving it to him to take out your shot. He may miss and take out his own. Should he take yours out, he will leave it easy for you to take both his rocks with your last stone, and you will count a good end.

22. Don't be greedy and attempt to count more shots especially when you are up on the score. Many games

are lost through greed. It is better to count two than take undue risks for a four—for a shot may miss by a hairline at any time no matter how good the player may be.

23. Don't get your guards too close, for your opponent may get both your guards and your shot. A fairly long guard is better than a close one.

24. Sometimes a lead's stone near the centre in front of the rings is good. Should your opponent leave it, or miss it, it is open for you to raise it to one side, and roll to the other side. Should he take it out, you can take his, and still get your roll to the side.

25. Remember, an opponent's rocks in front of the tee are more dangerous than those at the back.

26. It is often more advisable to keep your opponent from scoring than to take risky chances to win the end by one shot, especially when you are up in the score.

27. The better class rinks sometimes play for a dead end rather than count only one shot with their last rock which would again be theirs on the next end. This is based on the theory that your players will set up a better end, and count more next time.

28. A lead's or second's rock half way over the hog-line is often a disconcerting obstruction to the opponents when they have the last rock. If left in position, you are afforded a chance to get a stone in the rings behind it, which may win you the end.

29. The better rinks are versatile in their style of game and may start out with one style, which if not effective, will be switched to another style. Later, they may revert to the original style.

30. The standing of the score is also a determining factor. If you are up a few points, it is an indication that your style is O.K. If you are down, something is wrong with it. All this is, of course, based on the assumption that the two rinks are equally good.

31. With versatile rinks competing, it is sometimes advantageous to use one style: say the draw, until you have a good lead. Then, if you are sure of your players, you can switch to the hit game to prevent your opponents

from scoring by upsetting their draw game. The danger in
this strategy is that your players may be off their hit
game, which might give your opponents a good end. In
such an event, you would have to revert to the draw
game, which might require you to waste an end before
you could get your touch back for the draw. Games
have been lost because the skip didn't switch his style.
Games have been lost because he did switch, but his
players could not make the shots. Nevertheless, it is
the versatile rink with its call for skill, the element of
danger, the action and excitement, which has become
the ambition of most curlers.

32. A rink ought to be able to take a gamble once in a
while, for there are times when there is a safe shot to
count one, and a possible gamble for four or five. Should
the game be in the early stages, it is worth a chance on
the basis of: "This shot made once in five times equals
five points which is equal to a single point made on each
of five ends." If the odds are greater than the possible
score, the gamble should not be taken. Of course, should
a rink be down in the score, chances have to be taken,
but if up one point or more, the single point is taken,
and your lead protected.

33. Remember, there is a time for the draw shot and a time
for faster ones. Often a draw to "seize" to shot rock will
win the game, but skill is required to do it.

34. Don't be discouraged if you are down 10 points with
half the game over—remember, a game is not won until
the last stone—and your opponents may become over-
confident and grow careless, which will give you your
chance.

It should not be assumed that this resumé represents
more than the rudiments of the game of curling or that
after absorbing the section concerning "playmaking and
skipping", the reader can qualify as skip. "Top Flight" curlers and Class A skips are not born, but are the product of
knowledge and experience.

## SIGNALS

It is a common practice amongst the ordinary ranks of players to shout and bawl instructions. This leads to confusion with the result that the player often does not know what shot is being called for. Such conditions are not found when the better class of rink is playing. Although an experienced curler usually knows what is required without having to refer to the skip, the good rinks generally use a series of signals. The usual signals (made by the skip) are as follows:

*In-turn* — Right arm extended horizontally to the right.

*Out-turn* — Left arm extended horizontally to the left.

A *Guard* — The ice is patted with the broom where the guard is to stop.

*Draw Shot* — The broom is drawn along the ice in a curve towards the place where the stone should stop.

*Taken Out Shot* — The rock to be taken out is patted. The broom is swung backward if a fast running shot is required. If the shot to be taken out is to be hit on the side for a roll or a wick, the side of the rock to be hit is patted.

*Draw Wicks* — The broom is passed along the side of the rock on which the wick is to be made.

*To Seize A Shot* — The broom is drawn along the ice to the shot and the ice is patted in front of it.

A *Slow Stone* — The broom is held up horizontally to remind the player that the rock must not exceed a certain distance.

*Indicating An Opponent's Rock* — The broom is held in an inverted position over the opponent's rock. The broom is held in a vertical position over one of your own stones.

*To Sweep* — The skip starts to sweep in front of himself.

*To Stop Sweeping* — The skip holds up his hand or broom.

The skip's broom, of course, provides the direction line for the player, allowing for the rock's curl or curve. The required angular correction in the stone's direction line is given by the skip, who places his broom for the player to aim and swing at. The correction allowance given by the broom varies with the type of shot and with the speed required, less ice being given with the broom for fast shots, more for medium speed shots, and still more for draw shots and guards. It is necessary for the player to know what speed (weight) to use for the broom allowance given by the skip. While players with some experience will know the weight required from the allowance given by the skip's broom, the skip must inform the inexperienced ones. The general terms used are:—

Draw weight                —slow, to stop in front rings
Tee weight                 —to reach the Tee line
Back ring weight           —to reach the back rings behind the
                             Tee
Hack weight                —fast enough to reach the hack
Back board weight          —fast enough to reach the end of the
                             ice
Full weight                —as much speed as possible without
                             losing direction

Skips should use the edge of the broom to give the ice. Giving the flat of the broom is not sufficiently accurate because the broom is 12 inches or more in width, and 1 inch off the line of direction will miss the shot.

# CHAPTER III

# AN ANALYSIS OF THE ART OF CURLING

## By H. E. Weyman

### Physical and Mental Characteristics Required

1. A good sense of equilibrium or balance. This is necessary in delivery.

2. A sense of rhythm, or a lack of muscular tension.

3. Determination, a willingness to spend time practising, learning, and perfecting the delivery of the stone.

4. Ability to concentrate. Curling requires this quality as much as golf or any other game.

5. Fortitude and courage. No good curler is mentally licked until the last stone is thrown.

6. Self-confidence but *not* conceit: You must have confidence in your own ability to execute a shot whether it be hard or easy.

7. Co-operative spirit, comradeship — curling is even more than "Team-Play", it is "Unit-Play". There is no place for a Hitler or a Mussolini in it. You must have confidence in your team mates and your skip. No rink wants a crab.

8. Relax—the ability to relax—or the mental approach— plays a very important part. Don't let a lucky shot by the opposition *rattle* you. You'll get your share of lucky shots. Concentrate on the proper delivery, speed, and relaxation and you will be making the shots necessary for a win.

Curling has several fundamentals. The two basic ones are:

1. Line of direction.

2. Speed.

If both are correct, the shot will be 100 per cent perfect. The problem is, therefore, one of consistently obtaining direction and speed.

## THE HACK AND DIRECTION

The "hack" is the starting point of the line of direction, the broom is the finishing point, and the distance between is approximately 114 feet. The line of direction is almost invariably at an angle to the centre line of the ice and rings.

To obtain direction, the side of the "hack" or delivery position next to the centre line of the ice should be 3 inches from that centre line. Should the measurement be less, the stone cannot be delivered from the centre line, except by unnaturally twisting knees and legs. This results in tension and slight movement of the body from the centre position of delivery, which is sufficient to cause many shots to be missed. The shape of the toe hole of the "hack" is also important. It should be 3½ inches wide and about 5½ inches in length to permit the foot and toe to point straight up the ice without twisting the knee or ankle.

## DELIVERY OF THE CURLING STONE

Although not nearly enough stress is laid on the "delivery", or throwing of the curling stone, yet it is the most vital and important thing in the play of each individual curler, for upon it depends his skill and success as a curler and his enjoyment of the game. What the golf swing is to the golfer, so is the "delivery swing" to the curler. On the golf course one sees dozens of players practising by the hour. In the curling club you will not see one in thirty doing any practising at all. The golfer realizes that practice is necessary to gain proficiency. The curler seems to think that no matter how he sprawls his way out of the hack he will possibly make the shot for which the skip is calling. But it doesn't work out that way consistently. The golfer's chief thrill is to hit that pill smoothly and drive it a country mile or more accurately. The curler's chief thrill is concerned with throwing the rock smoothly and accurately.

The graceful pose caught by this picture emphasizes perfect rhythm and beautifully timed delivery. The important features are the straight arm following the stone, and complete freedom and relaxation, essential to a skilful curler.

This divergence of thought and purpose in two such closely related sports is hard to account for. As in every sport, an allowance must be made for the unorthodox guy, who, through some freak of nature, (or years of heart-breaking practice and experience) manages to get away with everything short of murder. Prospective curlers will save many headaches and much time by adopting orthodox methods and sound mechanics such as described here.

There are three distinct methods in general use of delivering the curling stone:

1.  The Push Delivery, the NEMESIS of curling, where the stone is pushed along the ice to obtain the required distance. The player uses little or no swing, and moves forward as far as he can reach, and then pushes the stone with his arm and hand under tension. Some players who use a swing, also push the rock by means of tightening up the arm and hand at the end of the swing, while others who use a slide, slide along with the rock, and, at the end of the slide, give it a shove. This type of delivery has been the ruination of many potentially fine curlers, and has prevented others from ever attaining sufficient skill to appreciate and enjoy curling.

2.  The Stationary Swing Delivery: This is the original and orthodox method, used by more or less skilful curlers. With this delivery a moderate swing is used with little or no slide. The weight of the stone is felt or caught as the swing comes forward, and with the body and shoulders held back, the rock is swung forward with a slight heave from the shoulder. The body, arm and hand, completely relaxed, follow after the stone. In recent years the accuracy and skill of this delivery has been improved through the use of the "balanced-swing" and "foot-pivot".

3.  The Balanced Swing-Slide Delivery: With its graceful action is not only responsible for the remarkable advancement in skill and ability, but has proved sufficiently intriguing to entice the younger generation to adopt the game. This delivery is made under complete relaxation, using the "balanced-swing" and the "foot-pivot". The momentum gained by the full swing, together with the power produced by the "balanced foot-pivot" is utilized to obtain the necessary speed, and also the long sliding follow-through. When this type of delivery is properly mastered, there is no push or shove to obtain speed or slide, the whole delivery being a smooth rhythmical action. The picture below gives an idea of the graceful style, but the broom is held too high.

The "Balanced Stationary Swing-Delivery"

The illustration above, showing the "Balanced Stationary Swing-Delivery", and the illustration on the following page showing the "Balanced Swing-Slide Delivery", both picture top notch curlers in action, and their individual techniques merit careful examination. Note that in the first illustration the rock is "swung" utilizing a throw or heave from the shoulder. Note, too, the use of the modern "Foot Pivot" on the hack, the foot pointing straight up the centre line. On the following page examine the long, graceful slide, the "Finger Tip Control", and the complete relaxation of arm and hand in the Follow Through. The necessary speed, of course, is secured by the amount of the Back Swing.

THE "BALANCED SWING-SLIDE DELIVERY"

The "balanced-swing" and the "'foot-pivot" are component parts of the delivery. The "balance" is obtained by placing almost all the weight on the right foot; the left serving only to maintain balance. For the "foot-pivot", the ball of the right foot, which points straight up the centre line, is placed on the edge of the hack on which it pivots in conjunction with the swing and forward movement. See diagram on the facing page.

The weight and pressure, applied to the foot angle or fulcrum, create a source of power propulsion available for use in conjunction with the momentum gained from the swing, to secure the desired speed and slide.

The potential power in the swing can be visualized at position "A". The angles formed between the body and upper limb during the swing have an important bearing on power poten-

tial, speed and control. To secure the proper angle on the
back swing with the body pitched as shown in position "A"
on the diagram, necessitates the player rising sufficiently
from the hack position. Never attempt to lean or bend beyond
the slight forward pitched position in the hack when the
stance is taken and don't kick yourself out of hack to follow
through. As the swing continues forward the angle increases
and flattens out as the stone is released. Failure to rise
sufficiently from the hack position is one of the most common
faults, for then the tail of the player is too high. This results in
loss of power, speed and control, inducing the player to push
the stone in an attempt to remedy the deficiency.

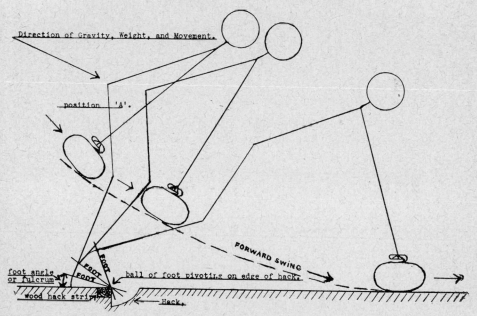

## The Essentials and Mechanics of the Delivery

Before describing the stance, it is necessary to state that
there are two distinct and separate ones, the SIDE or
ANGULAR STANCE, which is not recommended, and the
STRAIGHT LINE STANCE:

A. The side or angular stance is where the player's foot rests
   sideways in the hack or at an angle to the centre line. In
   this instance the player must twist his ankle and knee if
   his shoulders and upper part of the body are to face

squarely up the ice in order to permit the delivery swing
to be parallel with the centre line. (See illustration). This
posture is unnatural and induces stiffness and tension due
to the twisted position of the lower limb. In order to
relieve the tension the great majority of players turn the
body and shoulders at an angle to the centre line which
results in the delivery swing being made from an angle.
The effect is loss of accuracy and control. The use of the
Side Stance also eliminates the use and advantage of the
"Foot-Pivot" which cannot function.

SIDE OR ANGULAR STANCE

B. The straight line stance is more modern and it is obtained
by placing the foot in the hack to point straight up the
centre of the ice. In this position the entire body is facing
up the ice without tension permitting the delivery swing
to be made parallel to the centre line, thus securing greater
accuracy with less effort. This type of stance possesses the
important advantages of the "foot-pivot" previously described.

THE MECHANICS

1. The Stance:
   First, take up position in the "hack" by placing the ball of
   your foot squarely on the back of the "hack", toe pointing
   straight up the ice, parallel with the centre line. Then sit
   down on your right heel with your left foot flat on the

ice just beside your right, with left knee well bent forward. The weight of your body (your balance) should be kept well to the rear, as if you were sitting down on your heels. Keep your body upright with head and chin up, and eyes looking straight ahead.

Hold your stone lightly with fingers and extend right arm as far forward as it can comfortably go without changing the position of the body. You should now feel solid and comfortable. The practice of some curlers of sliding out the left foot and stretching the body out in front of the hack to aim the stone before the delivery swing is commenced, is wasted motion, dangerous, and entirely unnecessary, and likely to result in loss of balance, direction and rhythm. Therefore, retain your position in the hack and aim at the broom.

For the "Balanced Delivery" be sure you have your broom in your left hand, which, by the way, should be extended to the side (like a tight-rope walker) to help maintain balance.

Start your back swing from this position. Keep your right knee off the ice. No preliminary wagging or jerking or swaying forward. Just start the back swing slowly from the position described.

2. The Grip:

The *grip,* or taking hold of the handle of a curling stone, is an important factor in skilful curling. Take hold of the handle of the stone with the four fingers only, the thumb resting lightly on the side near the top. If this is properly done, the handle will lie across the fingers when the arm is extended, just like the golf club does, with the fingers holding the handle sufficiently firm but flexible, without muscular tension. The palm of the hand should not touch the handle at any time during the delivery. To attain these features of the grip, the better-class curlers use the "hand-lock" method shown in pictures Nos. 1 and 2. Picture No. 1 gives the first position of the grip where the handle is lying across the four fingers with the palm open. Now, turn the hand and wrist over to the left or counterclockwise until the thumb rests against the side of the handle—see picture No. 2. The handle is *now* locked in the hand, so to speak, without muscular tension or gripping tight, similar to the proper method of holding a golf club. This grip enables the player to acquire "Finger Tip Control", that sensitive touch or feel possessed by the best curlers and so essential for accuracy of distance and direction. Never take hold of the handle too near the goose-neck for the rock will then be unbalanced, causing it to tip during the swing and to hit the ice on the forward swing. You will also lose the line of direction. Be careful never to grip the handle tightly with the fist for it places you under tension and encourages a "push delivery". Picture No. 2 also illustrates the position of the hand and arm before the back swing is commenced, and again, the position of the hand at the finish of the delivery, just before the stone slides out of the fingers.

1.                                                   2.

THE PROPER HOLD OR GRIP

First position of the hand-lock        Second or final position showing
grip.                                handle locked in fingers.

3. Putting the Turn or Spin on the Stone:
While the turn (spin) is put on the stone during the forward swing (see illustration further on) preparation is made for it after the stance has been taken and the stone properly held. The stone is placed on the centre line and delivered from the centre line. Make no mistake about that! For the in-turn the handle is set straight or parallel with the centre line, the goose-neck pointing forward up the ice, the end of the handle pointing to the rear. For the out-turn the handle is set at an angle across the line with the tip or end of the handle pointing to the left towards the player. This has proved the best of all methods used to obtain an accurate out-turn delivery.

The proper amount of turn or spin is when the stone makes 3 to 4 complete turns during its course from end to end and which produces the maximum amount of curl and possible run or distance. Too much turn or spin stops the curl and shortens the natural run or distance which the stone would otherwise have; for the stone will be forced out of its natural run and will cut or drag the ice. While there are exceptions, the importance of the proper amount of turn is little realized although it is the cause of much confusion and misjudgment by both skips and players, and many lost games due to inability to judge the curl and run of the different players' stones.

Note: Many players have trouble in mastering the out-turn. This could be avoided or corrected if they held the handle at an angle across the line of play, as already described. The majority of the more skilful curlers use the method illustrated by the two pictures Nos. 3 and 4 given below. Picture No. 3 shows the position of the hand and the handle before commencing the back swing. This position is obtained by taking hold of the handle as described in paragraph 2 and photographs 1 and 2. After obtaining the position as shown in No. 2, turn the handle of the rock at an angle towards the left, see picture No. 3. The grip is not changed from that shown in picture No. 2, but the turning of the wrist to obtain the angle opens the palm of the hand as illustrated in picture No. 3. The rock is now drawn back on the back swing. On the forward swing, the wrist turns slowly without tension to the right or counter-clockwise. The "turn" automatically occurs just before the rock is soled on the ice. Picture 4 illustrates the position as the rock is about to leave the fingers. With this style, the wrist will turn naturally with the weight for the out-turn, and the fingers cannot get hooked in the goose-neck when the stone slides out of the hand with the fingers and thumb in control. It also permits finger tip control until the rock has left the hand. It is the light pressure of the thumb on the side of the handle pressing it against the fore-finger, which transmits the sense of distance and control to the player's brain.

3.                                          4.

THE PROPER "OUT-TURN" HOLD OR GRIP

The first position.            Final position before rock leaves
                                          the fingers.

4.  The Essential Mechanics of the Swing:
    The actual delivery of the stone is made by the swing,
    the mechanics of which are very similar to the golf swing.
    Those who have studied and learned the golf swing will
    easily appreciate the following:

    The swing is divided into two parts, namely:

       A.  The Back Swing.

       B.  The Forward Swing.

    A.  The Back Swing: This is one of the two most
        important phases of the delivery, just as it is in the
        golf swing. With almost all your weight on the
        right foot, draw your stone back from the stance
        position. Be sure to keep your body upright with
        your shoulders squarely facing the rings at the
        other end of the ice sheet and don't allow your
        weight to lean forward. The position of the body,
        shoulders, and head do not change at all during the
        entire swing. This fact is vital. The swing is made
        from the shoulder joint, similar to the pendulum
        of a hall clock. The right knee now straightens,
        elevating the body (not too high—see diagram with
        notes) the left moves backward to the side for
        balance, but the body remains squarely facing the

ice sheet with the head and chin up and eyes looking along the line of direction, all free of tension.

Remember all movements during the complete swing, back and forward, must be strictly parallel with the direction line. No sway or side motion of the body or head. Always be careful not to permit the shoulder to drop or lower on account of the weight of the rock. To attain a rhythmical arc the the rock must be raised sufficiently to clear the ice at the commencement of the swing and swung back to the "point of weight" where the player is able to sense or feel the weight.

It is essential to skilful curling that the player should sense the point of weight which cannot be attained with a short, insufficient swing or a fast swing. For a draw shot, the back swing should be just sufficient to reach the "point of weight". For faster shots increase the arc of the swing to gather more weight. Remember to start the swing slowly and easily and to obtain both the timing and rhythm. Don't get into the habit of taking the same back swing, no matter how fast or slowly a shot is to be played, for you will likely push the stone in order to give it the necessary speed, this will probably spoil the shot. Remember: no "pusher" gets the broom direction consistently, and this also applies to the player who attempts to hold the rock back, to obtain less speed and distance.

B. The Forward Swing: At the top of the back swing the stone in your fingers is hanging like a pendulum from the shoulder joint, and has to reverse its direction. It is at this point that the sense of weight must be achieved for the distance required. Therefore, keep the shoulders, body and head still, and begin the forward swing slowly and smoothly. At the same time, be sure to hold yourself, and your weight *back*, for the swing to come through. As the right arm moves forward with the swing, turn the wrist slowly (not the arm or shoulder) *in* for the in-turn, or *out*, for the out-turn, so that the handle and stone are turning when the player lets the stone go. This must take place near the end of the forward swing (not before) and be completed just before the stone contacts the ice. If the player neglects these essentials he will either have to put the turn on after the stone has contacted the ice, which encourages a "push delivery", or the twist he gives the handle will throw the stone off the line of direction. Again, putting the turn on too early in the forward swing will likely cause the stone to be released *too soon*, resulting in loss of distance and direction. Last but not least, never attempt to use the shoulder, hand or body to get the distance or the turn of the stone. It is essential that you use the natural momentum of the swing with its centrifugal force, or stored energy. So keep that body out of the delivery swing. Swing from the shoulder but don't let it turn or move.

5.  The Modern Parallel Delivery Swing:
    The entire delivery is a streamlined parallel motion of all body movements, the body and shoulders always retaining the right angle position to the centre line of the ice. Any swaying or movement, even of the head during the swing, will affect the shot adversely. The correct angle for direction to the broom is secured with the arm during the forward part of the swing, and not by changing or moving the position of body or shoulders while in the hack, or by making the backswing with a semi-circular motion of the shoulders. These basic mechanics are of such importance as to warrant the diagram: The Modern Parallel Delivery Swing which demonstrates:

1.  the square position of the body across the ice sheet during the complete swing,

2.  that the back swing is parallel with the centre line of the ice,

3.  that the maximum angle of the arm in relation to the centre line, to obtain direction to a broom giving 6' borrow, is astonishingly small, only 3½° and that the direction line to a broom giving 6' borrow, is only 6½ inches to either side of the centre line at the Tee nearest the player—(12' in front of hack). If the basic mechanics of this Parallel Delivery are adhered to, the problem of obtaining consistent accuracy is simplified, with the resultant improvement in skill and ability. The direction line which the player in the diagram is taking, would with tee weight, hit the sideboards at or near the hog line.

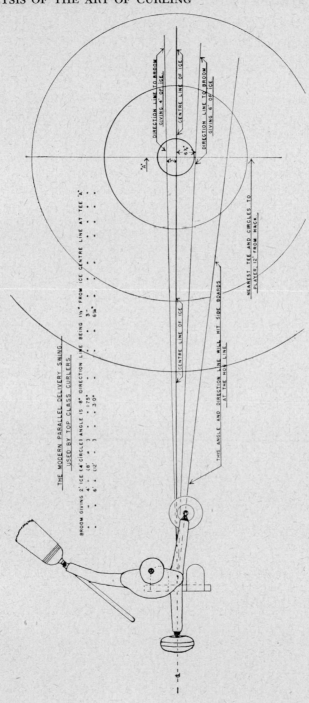

*Rhythm:* This is just as essential to the entire swing of a skilful curler as it is to the low handicap golfer and can be described as a smooth, even flowing, effortless, symmetrical motion of the swing, with body movements in perfect co-ordination. This is intriguing to watch. It cannot be acquired without practice, and freedom of tension is essential. The player must "give in" freely to the momentum of the swing, in other words, allow the momentum of the swing to swing you forward to follow after the stone. Any attempt to stiffen up, hold back or check the natural sequence of motion necessary to complete the swing and the subsequent follow through, will affect the shot adversely. To secure the full benefit of the rhythm and timing, many of the best curlers after delivering the rock at the hack allow themselves to slide out after the stone. Rhythm is a vital element in consistently skilful curling.

*The Straight Arm:* Be careful to keep a straight and relaxed arm during the forward swing and until the stone has left the fingers. Don't allow the arm to bend at the elbow or you will get a hook delivery, usually with an "out-turn". If the arm is bent you cannot consistently "get the broom" even with an in-turn. Your eyes should be looking along your arm on the direction line to the broom during the follow through.

*Keeping the Rock Ahead:* Curlers and also golfers are more adversely affected by this feature of the mechanics than by any other. The tendency is in both cases to use the body, shoulders, and legs, instead of the natural swing. In golf the cry is "'hold back" or stay behind the ball, and the same applies to the curler. In golf should your body lead the club head, something other than a good shot will result. It is the same with curling. Don't let the body lead the rock. Always allow the swing and the stone to come through ahead of the body, especially when the rock is about to make contact with the ice. Make sure you fully complete the swing before allowing yourself to slide forward to follow the "delivered" rock. In other words, keep the body and shoulders out of the swing, otherwise you will not succeed in making the shots you should.

Again, using the golf comparison, if the golfer were to stand perfectly still and hit the ball with hands and arms only, he would hit a straight and true ball most of the time but with little distance. To execute the proper golf swing merely requires the player to keep his body from interfering. Of course, the trick is to do it.

The same thing applies to the curling "delivery" and swing. For if you stand flat-footedly on the hack, squat (not lean) down till you can reach the handle of the rock in such position that the stone can hang from the shoulder, in a straight line with your body, chest up, you can lift the stone with your leg muscles. If you can follow these gyrations, stay flat-footedly in the hack and keep your body absolutely still. Now let your arm slowly swing the stone back. Bring it forward (keep the body still) and let it go without moving your feet off the hack. If you do this you may have thrown the rock but a few feet, but you have properly delivered a stone and have "stayed behind" it. It's as simple as that. Of course, to throw it to the other end of the ice and keep the body from interfering and still have a nice sliding "follow through", takes practice. If you'll try this flat-footed idea enough times you may get the "feel" of being behind the stone. It would seem that there's a sort of killer instinct in all of us, for the most overpowering desire seems to be that of starting the body toward the shot first. The stone just never has a chance to catch up. The same thing applies to the golf swing. You must never overlook the essential factor of fully completing the swing before allowing the body to follow. In other words, "let the delivery swing, swing you forward".

Remember in curling they say "Get the broom and the weight, and you'll get the shot". The only way to get the broom consistently is to swing the stone towards the broom, allowing your arm to reach out ahead of your body and follow the stone (follow through). That means you must put the turn (spin) on the stone near the end of the swing before it is soled on the ice.

*The Follow Through:* Again, like golf and some other sports, the "follow-through" is vital. Many players who neglect or fail to comply with other essentials are able to play a fair game at times on account of their follow-through, but they will always remain in their class with no hope of improvement unless they master the other essentials. The "follow-through" commences after the stone has passed the legs on the forward swing and has contacted the ice. As the stone comes down to contact the ice, the body comes down after it, as close to the ice as possible. The arm, straight and relaxed with no pressure on the handle (finger tip control) follows the stone along the line of direction to the broom (see the various pictures). The closer the body finishes to the ice, the easier it is to attain accurate direction. The entire motion on the forward swing is similar to the graceful, gliding motion of a bird alighting on the ground.

The picture depicts the square position of the body across the ice at this stage of the follow through slide, the straight arm, the slow turn on the rock, the eyes fixed on the broom and the mind concentrated on distance and weight required. The hand does not fly up in the air.

As the "follow-through" continues, the speed of the player's slide becomes less than the speed of the rock, and the handle being lightly held with a straight arm finally glides out of the fingers. With the true finger tip control the player can feel the handle gently caress the fingers as the rock glides away.

There is no push, no effort, no tension in either hand, arm or body, all of which must follow the rock along the direction line. It is of the utmost importance to complete the "follow through" and it is also important that the player should not rise, or jump up before it is properly completed. Don't let the hand and arm fly upward into the air when releasing the stone, for you will likely exert pressure on the handle and lose direction. Remember, the slide is longer for draw shots and guards.

THE FINISH OF A PERFECT DELIVERY

The important feature of this picture is the low position with the eyes aimed down the straight and relaxed arm along the direction line. Note that the hand does not fly up in the air.

*The Sliding "Follow Through":* Sliding out with the "follow through" undoubtedly assists in obtaining a perfect rhythmical delivery without tension or effort, but sliding for considerable distances is not essential.

The essential point is to avoid any action, or tension, which might obstruct, or stop the momentum of the swing, and forward movement of the player which makes it essential that a free and complete "follow through" be achieved. This is just as vital in curling as it is in the golf swing. It is purely a question of what length of slide secures freedom and the confidence of the player. Some curlers are able to achieve it with very little sliding, others with more slide, yet others with a long slide.

According to the exponents of the lengthy slides, the chief advantage gained is complete relaxation and freedom of forward movement without interruption, the player being behind the rock and following it. One of the chief difficulties of most players is allowing the body to get ahead of the rock. This is not likely to happen if a sufficient slide, or a long slide is taken. The long slide is obtained through removing the rubber from the left foot, or sliding on the heel, or side of the foot.

## Possible Physical Handicaps

For players, who for physical reasons, are unable to get down to the ice on the forward swing, it is absolutely essential that the body, head and shoulders are kept squarely facing up the ice without change during the entire swing, including the "follow through". They must follow through as far as possible. Any movement of the body, shoulders or head will throw the stone off line. Use the stationary swing delivery.

## A Sequence of Photographs Illustrating Correct Delivery Technique

The various stages in the correct delivery technique are illustrated in the sequence of photographs on the next five pages. The player, of course, is an acknowledged expert. He is using the "Balanced Swing-Slide Delivery".

A Comfortable position—Taking a comfortable and relaxed position in the hack. The feet are close together with the left knee well bent forward permitting the player to be lower and more comfortable. The left arm with broom is well extended to obtain relaxation of the trapezius muscle.

Aim at the broom—Right arm with stone is extended towards broom, but not sufficient to place any strain or tension    body, or to cause any movement of body or legs from original position.

BACK SWING—The back swing commences. Position of feet has not altered. Body has risen but retains its position. Weight has commenced to come on the right leg. Incidentally keeping weight on right leg reduces chances of slipping to a minimum. Slipping on the ice occurs when there is too much weight on left foot.

BACK SWING CONTINUES—Stone is now almost level with the legs and weight is all on right leg. Left foot starts to move to the left to maintain balance. Left arm and broom is well extended just as is done when carrying a bucket of water and promotes relaxation and balance.

Top of back swing—Weight all on right foot, balance is maintained by left foot. The body, although raised, retains its original position facing squarely up the ice. The amount of the back swing varies according to the speed at which you want the stone to travel. In the opinion of some critics both body and stone are raised too much in this picture.

Forward swing and turn—The stone is passing the legs on the forward swing and is AHEAD of the body and the turn is being put on. The left foot is actually off the ice and moving forward to position in front which causes the figure to seem ungainly. Actually the body and head still retain their original poise.

RHYTHM—The stone with the turn on has not yet touched the ice but is well ahead of the body. Note the smooth way the stone is going to meet the ice surface. The body is still facing squarely up the ice sheet.

STONES SLIDES OUT OF THE HAND—With the body still facing squarely up the ice, the stone with the turn already on, has slid out of the hand. The actual delivery has been completed and the follow through has commenced. The left arm and broom are well behind inducing complete relaxation.

FOLLOW THROUGH CONTINUES—The stone is more than two feet over the Tee Line. The player is sliding on his left heel and side of right foot. Some players obtain a long slide by leaving off the rubber of the left foot or by using the toe or with the ball of the foot, while others deliver the stone with little or no slide at all. The object is: to obtain complete relaxation, no push, or pressure, on the handle of the stone.

THE SLIDING FOLLOW THROUGH—Although the stone is well on its way, the player allows himself to continue sliding right through the rings. The purpose is to obtain a rhythmical delivery and relaxation. However, long sliding is not essential, but a proper Follow-Through is vital.

## A Warning

Many a young curler, and even those who have been playing the game for some time, have ruined it by attempting a long slide with the "follow through", the reason being that he takes a long slide by pushing off from the "hack", then when he is out on slippery ice, sliding along with the stone under him (not ahead), gives the stone a push towards the broom. In this case, the player has not delivered the rock from the hack but from the end of his slide and is, therefore, illegal. He is also ahead of the rock as he pushes off from the hack before the swing and delivery have been completed. In the true sliding delivery the rock is swung and "delivered towards the broom at the hack", and the curler follows many feet after it until the stone slides out of his hand. Recognition of these points in the delivery of the rock is not generally understood. There is all the difference in the world between a curler whose swing takes place in the hack, and who then follows after it, to the one who pushes off and rides his stone as he slides, and then pushes it at the end of the slide.

## AN ABBREVIATION OF THE PRINCIPAL ESSENTIALS

1. Relaxation: Keep yourself free of tension in mind, body, arms, etc. Don't run to the "hack" and hurriedly deliver your stone, and don't make yourself uneasy by thinking that you may miss the shot. Think only of delivering that stone right.

2. Stance in the "hack": Try to take the proper stance and make yourself feel comfortable. Note the line of direction to the broom. Avoid looking at the shot itself if you are drawing to it, or taking it out. Fix your eyes on the broom and concentrate your thought and sense on the swing and weight required.

3. Think of the speed and weight you require.

4. Remember to keep the body and shoulders and head facing the rings squarely. Swing the stone like a pendulum.

5. Lift and swing the stone slowly and easily back, drawing the left foot back and to the left side at the same time, allowing your weight to come on your right leg.

6. Adjust the length of your back swing for the speed required.

7. Still facing squarely up the ice, commence the forward swing slowly and smoothly.

8. Put the turn on the stone during the forward swing just before the stone touches the ice.

9. Be sure the stone is ahead of the body when it touches the ice.

10. Complete the forward swing by following right through as far as you can reach to the broom without disturbing the square position of the body, etc., and without any pressure on the handle of the stone as it leaves your fingers. Don't draw up your right leg until the "follow through" is completed. Keep it out behind you and it will help your balance.

11. Don't follow through with a rising body. In other words, don't start raising the body until the "follow through" has been completed.

12. Never use your body, shoulder or hand to obtain speed or turn on the stone.

## SWEEPING

Many a curler is puzzled over the fact that the best skips will seem to choose inferior players in preference to better general players, who are indifferent sweepers. A large percentage of curlers consistently ignore the importance of being good sweepers, even though it means many lost games. Sweeping is an essential part of curling and fully recognized by all curlers west of the Province of Quebec. The Art of Sweeping has been highly developed in Western Canada, where it has become graceful and attractive to spectators. It is amusing, but also pitiful, to watch Easterners sweep beside the Western sweepers.

There are some who seem to be under the impression that the sole object of sweeping is to keep curlers warm, or awake, while others, again, think their stones are the only ones which should be swept.

Proper and efficient sweeping is an asset to any rink and has been developed into a graceful Art, which, if mastered, will be a source of pride and pleasure both to the player and the rink.

1. The broom ought to be light in weight with longer corn than the standard broom, and a thicker handle of soft wood. The length should be adjusted to the height of the player by cutting the handle. Several broom manufacturers supply special curling brooms.

2. It is held in a certain manner, the right hand at the top with the thumb resting on the handle pointing up; the left hand down the handle to act as a pivot point, while the right hand and arm moves back and forth, making the corn slap the ice each time. Many fine sweepers place the left hand underneath the handle palm to the front with the thumb resting on the handle point down. This gives more purchase power with less effort, particularly if the sweeper is on the left of the stone.

3. The sweeper moves in a line with the stone and behind the broom, which sweeps across the line of direction in front of him and the stone. It is contrary to the rules of curling and definitely illegal to sweep in the same direction that the stone is travelling. Don't forget this, you may lose a protest made against you for the infringement.

4. It is necessary to maintain complete relaxation in body, legs and arms, in order to move in complete co-ordination and rhythm. Give in like the dancer to the rhythm and sway, and you will not tire easily. The stiff and unresponsive sweeper tires quickly and his curling suffers in consequence.

5. Acquire the step or dance and sway of the real sweeper, and sweeping is no longer the hard labour of the chain gang.

6. With well-organized and co-ordinated rinks, it is customary for the player to follow his stone behind the sweepers. In this case, the player is in position at hog line to see the lay of the "House" for his next shot, and relieves the skip's voice and throat. Such team work has advantages,

and is general with rinks, whose players have played together over a period of time.

A real sweeper is a pleasure unto himself and a graceful attraction to the spectators.

The effect of sweeping has long been a controversial subject. For a considerable period, it has been claimed that the beautiful fast rhythmical sweeping of the Western curlers produces a vacuum in front of the moving stone, causing it to travel further than it otherwise would.

By means of a specially constructed apparatus, tests were made at two divergent points in Canada, both of which demonstrated that with proper and efficient sweeping a stone will travel 12 to 15 feet further than if it were not swept at all. This, in turn, means that a stone can be made to hold its course (run straighter) in order to get the shot which might otherwise be missed.

Recently, the author uncovered further proof of the effect of good efficient sweeping, which supports the experiments and study carried out by the Canadian experts. The tests in question were made at St. Moritz, Switzerland in 1924, and one or two of the tests are given herewith:—

### Authentic Sweeping Test

A number of actual tests were made at St. Moritz, Switzerland, in 1924, of the effect of sweeping a curling rock. While the curling rock used is somewhat lighter than the Canadian rock with a different cupping and bearing surface diameter, yet these tests definitely confirm the results, which were obtained at different points in Canada, where such tests were also carried out and support the statements made in this section of the Curling Analysis. The tests in Switzerland were made on an open air rink and under several weather conditions. In these tests the additional distance, which a curling rock will travel, when properly and efficiently swept, is more than what has been found in Canada. The principal point is that, although actual conditions were not the same, yet it was proved that proper sweeping will increase the distance travelled by a curling rock anywhere from 10′ to 18′. The details of the tests as carried out are given herewith:—

Test was made with the use of a sloping trestle, composed

of boards covered over with snow and then iced, the trestle
being sunk flush with the ice sheet and then finished off with
ice in order to provide a finished surface, which would permit the curling stone to slide down the plane and take the
level ice smoothly.

The same stone, of 36 lb. weight, with a cupping 120 m.m. in
diameter, 6 m.m. depth, and having a bearing surface 2 m.m.
wide, was used throughout in making the tests. Before each
trial the under surface of the stone was carefully cleaned.
The stone was held in position at a fixed point at the topmost
end of the inclined plane, and released without impetus to
slide by its own weight down the slope onto the ice, thereby
ensuring the same velocity and momentum each time. The
length of the resulting run was marked on the ice, and measured from the line of junction of plane and ice. With practice
it was possible to ensure the stone sliding down approximately
the same track. Any notable deviation from the track introduced a variable factor, and every trial in which the stone
failed to keep the track or failed to take the ice smoothly was
rejected. Repeated trials were made in order to obtain an
average length of run. The services were requisitioned of two
acknowledged experts in the art of vigorous sweeping.

TEST 1—January 13th, 1924: Ice moderately keen; fine day;
hot sun; height of starting point of stone on inclined plane
0.85 metres; length of plane 3.0 metres. Same stone used
throughout; in-handle turn; ice lightly swept before starting

| Trial | Distance run in Metres | Average Metres |
|---|---|---|
| 1. Unswept | 24.45 | |
| 2. Unswept, same track | 26.48 | |
| 3. Unswept, same track | 29.90 | |
| 4. Unswept, same track | 26.77 | 27.7 |
| 5. Unswept, same track | 28.60 | |
| 6. Unswept, same track | 29.98 | |
| 7. Stone swept all the way | 36.72 | 39.01 |
| 8. Stone swept all the way, same track | 42.20 | |
| 9. Stone sent down same swept track, not swept | 38.24 | 39.14 |
| 10. Stone sent down same swept track, not swept | 40.05 | |
| 11. Stone sent down same track and swept | 45.26 | 45.26 |

On moderately keen ice a gain in length of run of not less than 12 metres resulted from a vigorous sweeping. The same stone sent down the swept track, and not swept, ran as far (Nos. 9 and 10); further sweeping along the same track (No. 11) gave a further increase of 6 metres over the average of the two preceding unswept stones.

TEST II—January 15th, 1924: Fine day; clear sky; cross wind; very keen ice. Stone sent down from a point 0.52 metres high on the plane; length of run on plane 2.3 metres. (A lower starting point on the plane was used owing to the keenness of the ice; a stone sent down from the top over-ran the length of the rink.) Same stone used throughout; all in-handle shots; ice lightly swept before tests.

|  | Distance run in Metres |
|---|---|
| 1. Not swept | 26.68 |
| 2. Swept all the way | 30.28 |
| 3. Not swept, no turn | 25.10 |
| 4. Stone sent down from top of plane, not swept | 34.11 |
| 5. Ditto—swept (picked up a straw) | 39.00 |

On very keen ice sweeping resulted in a gain of 5 metres on an average run of 25 metres. On a longer run of 34 metres, when the stone was started from the top of the plane, sweeping gave an additional 12 metres, much the same result as in TEST I.

Advantage was taken of the plane to make certain further tests which proved interesting.
Does a stone, rotating slowly with a normal amount of "handle" on, curl more or less than a stone that is rotating rapidly with excess of handle? To test this point, four pairs of stones were used, the members of each pair having been proved to run equally. The first stone of each pair was sent down with a normal amount of handle (3 to 4 rotations from plane to tee) and the spot to which it curled marked on the ice. The second stone was then sent down the same track with excess of handle (7 to 13 rotations from plane to tee) and the spot to which it curled noted. The results are tabulated as follows:

TEST VI.—February 5th, 1924.

### Effect of Rotation

1st pair —1. Took  3 turns from slide to tee
           2. Took 13 turns from slide to tee and curled 4
               ft. less
2nd pair—1. Took  4 turns from slide to tee
           2. Took  8 turns from slide to tee and curled 4
               ft. less
3rd pair—1. Took  4 turns from slide to tee
           2. Took  7 turns from slide to tee and curled 2½
               ft. less
4th pair—1. Took 3½ turns from slide to tee
           2. Took 10 turns from slide to tee and curled 4
               ft. less

It is clear that a stone rotating slowly curls more than a twin stone rotating rapidly.

The distance that real sweeping will bring a rock is also dependent on temperature, ice pebble, ice conditions, and whether the player properly cleans the running surface of his rocks. Very important, too, is the condition of the broom. Curlers and Curling Clubs who desire to obtain long life and the best out of a good broom should hang or stand the broom up on the handle in the basement, or in a cool humid place. Don't leave it in the ice section or in a building where the broom corn will be constantly subjected to frost.

### A Sweeper's Responsibility

As soon as a player's rock crosses the first hog line it is in the charge of the sweepers, who bear the responsibility of seeing it safely to its destination. It is the duty of the sweepers, whether the stone has to be swept or not, to follow it in order to remove any loose straws or other impediments lying in the path of the moving rock. Any attempt to remove broom straws caught under the moving stone is direct interference and, therefore, an infringement of the rules. As the sweepers are responsible for keeping the path of the stone clear, it is their fault and neglect if straws are picked up by the stone.

SWEEPING WITH GRACE AND RHYTHM—The broom handles are cut to accommodate player's height, to permit right arm and hand to move level with the shoulder, not higher. The player in the rear is using the reverse grip, left hand under broom. The other player in front is using the front grip. Both players are well behind the travelling stone, sweeping in front of it and themselves. They are using the step dance, timed with the movement of the broom, producing both rhythm and grace of movement.

There is no rule which prevents the sweepers standing within the hog line next to the player, but the rock cannot be swept until after it has crossed the line. The player who is about to deliver the rock is generally expected to see that the ice is clear of any loose matter between the hack and the hog line.

Skips are responsible for keeping the rings clear of loose straws, etc. Should, however, a rock come to rest, which has caught up a straw, no attempt should be made to remove it without the consent of the opposing skip.

## FORMATION OF RINKS

Skilful clever curling rinks are usually formed by placing together players whose mental and personality characteristics co-ordinate, and where there is mutual appreciation and confidence. Remember in modern curling each player from the lead to the skip bears the same responsibility for the execution of any shot in the book and either one may be making the decisive shot of the game at any moment. This imposes pressure and strain on the human character and requires personal confidence and trust in each other. With well-knitted co-ordinated rinks each player becomes familiar with the ability and peculiarities of the other players and each automatically knows what the skip is likely to want and is familiar with the signals and tactics. The skip himself is well acquainted with the strong and weak points of each player and what he may expect from him. It is a source of pleasure as well as of lively interest to watch the quiet smooth play of a well co-ordinated team who proceed through the game without persistent shouting and bawling of instructions and information.

To reach the "ultimate" in curling, such rinks should be kept intact for several years.

# APPENDIX

## APPENDIX A

### Curling Clubs in Canada and the United States—1950*

| | | | |
|---|---|---|---|
| Alberta | 209 | P.E.I. | 4 |
| British Columbia | 32 | Quebec | 71 |
| Manitoba | 238 | Saskatchewan | 504 |
| New Brunswick | 21 | U.S.A. | 66 |
| Newfoundland | 2 | Yukon | 2 |
| North-West Territories | 11 | | |
| Nova Scotia | 31 | | |
| Ontario | 196 | **Total** | **1387** |

*This survey was carried out in the spring of 1950. It has not been possible to ascertain whether or not all unaffiliated clubs have been included.*

### Affiliated Ladies' Curling Clubs in Canada—1950*

| | | | |
|---|---|---|---|
| New Brunswick | 8 | P.E.I. | 1 |
| Newfoundland | 1 | Quebec | 39 |
| North-West Territories | 3 | Saskatchewan | 60 |
| Nova Scotia | 11 | | |
| Ontario | 19 | **Total** | **142** |

*Many ladies' clubs are not yet affiliated with the various associations.*

## APPENDIX B

### CURLING ASSOCIATIONS IN CANADA AND THE UNITED STATES — 1950

| | | |
|---|---|---|
| Alberta Branch R.C.C.C. | S. W. Foss | 532 - 14th Ave., N.E., Calgary, Alberta |
| Alberta Curling Association | J. M. McCool | Telephone Building, Edmonton, Alberta |
| British Columbia Curling Association | Geo. F. Reimann | Trail, British Columbia |
| Canadian Branch R.C.C.C. | R. E. Raguin | 1850 St. Luke Street, Montreal, Quebec |
| Crows Nest Pass Curling Association | E. W. Gibson | Fernie, British Columbia |
| Dominion Curling Association | W. B. Cowan, K.C. | 15 Toronto Street, Toronto, Ontario |
| Grand National Curling Club of America | Edwin W. Fiske, Jr. | Ardsley on Hudson, New York, U.S.A. |
| Manitoba Curling Association | R. F. O'Dowda | Donalda Block, Winnipeg, Manitoba |
| Midwest Curling Association | Joseph Carson | 225 East Mason Street, Milwaukee 2, Wisconsin |
| New Brunswick Branch R.C.C.C. | N. C. Ralston | Saint John, New Brunswick |
| Newfoundland Curling Association | P. G. Ledingham | St. John's, Newfoundland |

Northern Ontario Curling Association — C. A. Beach — Copper Cliff, Ontario

Northwestern Ontario Curling Association — T. C. Johnston — Port Arthur, Ontario

Northwestern Quebec Curlers Association — V. Killeen — Sigma Mines, Bourlamaque, Quebec

North West Territories Curling Association — A. W. Scott — Yellowknife, North West Territories

Nova Scotia Branch R.C.C.C. — P. A. Curry — 181 Bernard Street, New Glasgow, Nova Scotia

Ontario Curling Association — W. E. McMurtry — 42 Bernard Avenue, Toronto, Ontario

Peace River District and British Columbia Block Curling Association — W. E. McRae — Peau River, Alberta

Prince Edward Island Curling Association — J. F. MacLeod — Charlottetown, Prince Edward Island

Province of Quebec Curlers Association — H. E. Weyman — Box 100, Levis, Quebec

Saskatchewan Curling Association — I. Richardson — Mitchell Building, Regina, Saskatchewan

Selkirk Curling Association — Duncan MacDonald — Cranbrook, British Columbia

Temiskaming and Northern Ontario Curling Association — Don McKelvie — New Liskeard, Ontario

## APPENDIX C

## DOMINION CURLING ASSOCIATION

### MEMBERS[1]

| ASSOCIATION | 1948 - 1949 | | | 1949 - 1950 | | |
|---|---|---|---|---|---|---|
| | Clubs | Individuals | High School | Clubs | Individuals | High School |
| Alberta Branch | 80 | 5,489 | 1,500 | 85 | 5,654 | 300 |
| Alberta Curling | 113 | 8,459 | 3,000 | 88 | 6,790 | 4,500 |
| British Columbia | 21 | 2,175 | 200 | 21 | 2,175 | 200 |
| British Columbia Ladies | 9 | 310 | | 9 | 310 | |
| Crows Nest Pass | 4 | 293 | 37 | 4 | 300 | |
| Manitoba | 264 | 10,053 | 5,000* | 264 | 12,351 | 5,500 |
| New Brunswick Branch | 17 | 2,520 | 500 | 17 | 2,550* | 500 |
| New Brunswick Ladies | 8 | | | 8 | | |
| Newfoundland | 2 | 234 | | 2 | 340 | |
| Northern Ontario | 10 | 1,024 | 150 | 10 | 1,192 | 150 |
| Northern Ontario Ladies | | 220 | | | 280 | |
| North West Territories | 6 | 345 | 32 | 5 | 340 | 12 |
| North West Territories Ladies | 4 | | | 4 | | |
| Northwestern Ontario | 15 | 1,433 | | 16 | 1,425 | |
| Northwestern Quebec | 5 | 332 | 68 | 5 | 400 | 40 |

| | | | | | | |
|---|---|---|---|---|---|---|
| Nova Scotia | 24 | 2,590 | | 25 | 2,490 | |
| Ontario | 115 | 9,041 | | 116 | 10,500 | |
| Ontario Ladies | 17 | | | 18 | | |
| Peace River District & B.C. Block | | | | 32 | 2,000 | 500 |
| Prince Edward Island | 4 | 455 | 79 | 4 | 377 | 70 |
| Prince Edward Island Ladies | | | | 1 | | |
| Quebec | 14 | 1,850 | 80 | 15 | 1,750 | 300 |
| Quebec Ladies | 3 | | | 5 | | |
| Saskatchewan | 373 | 13,272 | 3,000 | 399 | 14,079 | 9,600* |
| Saskatchewan Ladies[2] | | | | | | |
| Selkirk | 5 | 386 | 60 | 5 | 448 | 20 |
| Selkirk Ladies | | | | 9 | | |
| Temiskaming & Northern Ontario | 16 | 1,782 | 300 | 16 | 1,782 | 100 |

*Approximate figures only.

[1] The foregoing statistics do not include all curling clubs or curlers in Canada for many clubs do not yet belong to the different Associations and many clubs do not report their full membership. In other cases no figures were available.

[2] The ladies' clubs of Saskatchewan have formed their own Association.

# INDEX